Waking Up

The Work of Charlotte Selver

Collected and Edited by
William C. Littlewood
with
Mary Alice Roche

authorHOUSE™

1663 LIBERTY DRIVE, SUITE 200
BLOOMINGTON, INDIANA 47403
(800) 839-8640
WWW.AUTHORHOUSE.COM

Table of Contents

Preface

In the 1940s Charlotte Selver (1901-2003) introduced to the United States the practice she called Sensory Awareness. In the 1920s and 1930s in Berlin she had been a student of the originators of this work: Elsa Gindler, a teacher originally of *Harmonische Gymnastik*, and Heinrich Jacoby, an innovative educator and musicologist.

Their thesis was a fundamental one. First, as healthy human beings, we are born with all possibilities for impression and expression. Second, if these possibilities do not develop, it is because we have been hindered by our early training. Finally, we can grow and change at any time through direct attention to what is happening in us in each moment as we move and breathe and go about whatever task presents itself. Countless people studied with these seminal teachers, and their pupils carried their work to no fewer than nine different countries.

Until January 2003, though hearing- and vision-impaired, Charlotte[1] continued to give workshops in the United States, in Europe, and in Mexico. Much like her teachers, Elsa Gindler and Heinrich Jacoby, Charlotte herself wrote practically nothing for publication. In keeping with the work they offered, their most telling words were spontaneous responses to class situations, to the actions and questions of their students. It is only in transcripts of their workshops over the years that one could find words coming somewhere near the essence of this basically experiential work.

As for Charlotte's interest in promoting in print her own work, for many years she allowed only a modicum of material to be published from the many tapes of her many classes. However, in 1974, her second husband and colleague, Charles V. W. Brooks, published his own account of her work in his *Sensory Awareness: The Rediscovery of Experiencing.*[2]

---

[1] "Charlotte" is how she referred to herself, and "Charlotte" is what all her students called her.

Another major break-through came in the early 1980s, when Charlotte herself asked me to make selections from the audio tapes of her classes for the purpose of publishing a book of her actual classroom comments and interactions.

I had by then studied with her for ten years or so and had been a member of her first long-term (nine-month) Study Group of 1972–1973. Even so, I was intimidated by the task. How was I to know what Charlotte considered important? How could I hear with her ears, see with her eyes? Worried and unsure, I had several consultations with her about this problem during those first months, but despite my doubts she was always encouraging, and at length she said, "Pick out what *you* think is important." With this mandate I settled down to reading through the available transcripts and listening to the many tapes. Over the ensuing years the resulting manuscript was compiled, revised, put away, resurrected, and gone over again and again with extensive editing help from Mary Alice Roche, who knew and had worked with Charlotte far longer than I, and with whom I collaborated on other editing projects over the years.

These tapes and transcripts cover more than two decades of Charlotte's workshops. Only for the classes transcribed in the *Appendices* are the dates and places given. The excerpted passages in the rest of the book come from many different classes given over a considerable number of years.

Given Charlotte's desire to find passages that would represent her teaching, it made no sense to me to present them separately or with endless footnotes. Thus, they have been arranged by topic (insofar as Sensory Awareness can be so arranged—it is, after all, a seamless work) in the hope of providing a text that would feel like Charlotte speaking and answering in a class session. The aim has been to represent the heart of her teaching as faithfully as possible, using only her own words. How

---

[2] Charles V. W. Brooks, *Sensory Awareness: The Rediscovery of Experiencing* (New York: The Viking Press, 1974). This was the original book. It was later reprinted as *Sensory Awareness: Rediscovery of Experiencing Through Workshops with Charlotte Selver* (Great Neck, NY: Felix Morrow, 1986). This book has been translated into German, Dutch, Spanish, and Japanese.

representative these selections are can only be a moot point: others might well have chosen differently. We hope there will be more and different representations of her work in future.

Charlotte's constant emphasis on practicing Sensory Awareness at any and all times in one's daily life has been her single most important lesson for me, and the time spent working on this manuscript has illuminated her teaching and impressed on me the subtlety and relevance of what she offers. I can now more easily trust myself to know when I am 'out of balance' and what to do about it. And, wonder of wonders, the habit of listening to what stirs in me keeps on growing. For me the bug has bitten, thanks to Charlotte.

This is a book about sensing. Sensing means taking the time, and being quiet enough inside, to become aware of what comes to us through all our senses. You may wish to try out some of the suggested experiments. These are highlighted in italic type. The ellipsis points between Charlotte's remarks signify long moments for silent attention. This, I believe, is all the preparation you need.

—William C. Littlewood
San Miguel de Allende, Mexico
August 2004

A Note on the Transcriptions

Charlotte Selver, née Wittgenstein, spoke German exclusively until she emigrated to the United States in 1938. Though she later acquired fluency in English, the interjections and syntax of her native German emerge again and again in the transcriptions of her classes. With charming regularity, for instance, she interjects "Ja," and just as often relies upon a syntactical construction of her own invention, "without that" (as in, ". . . without that you focus on anything . . ."). We have chosen to retain such irregularities, however mildly distracting to the reader, rather than silently correct or omit them altogether.

As one of her students remarked, Charlotte's "being her own English teacher" kept her students focused and expectant from one word to the next. Her unique syntax lent an air of unpredictability and of ever-unfolding newness to her classes. One could never presume to know what she would say next. Listening to her speak was much like hearing for the first time a new and different musical composition. For instance, Charlotte would seem to voice a simple observation: "Oh! A bird just flew by." A beat later, however, she would modulate her deep contralto voice to produce the query: "Could you feel it?"

As for Charlotte's voice as an instrument of her teaching, her students recall that she always spoke at a volume both natural to her and perfectly suited to her present environment. She must have had to adjust her voice to accommodate large classes and big spaces, but she never gave the impression of straining to project, of forcing her voice. In this respect, she was much like the singer who senses instinctively the sensitivities of her audience and the acoustics of her auditorium.

The reader will notice throughout the transcriptions the frequent asides [in brackets] denoting the laughter that erupted spontaneously during her classes. When something struck Charlotte herself as funny, her response was immediate: a hearty, full-throated chuckle—difficult to describe.

"Her communication came from something deep within her, to meet something deep within me," said one student. "I felt it personally, and, during the experiments, I always felt I had absolute freedom for my way of expression." Charlotte's voice was true to what she was feeling and true to what she was responding to in teaching Sensory Awareness.

REMEMBER ALWAYS THAT WHAT WE ARE DOING HERE, if it doesn't change your life it's worth nothing. If you take this as a kind of oasis to which you come and have a beautiful hour or two in which you kind of begin to breathe and live, and then you go into your life and act just the same, don't take the trouble. If it doesn't gradually change your life it doesn't go deep enough.

—Charlotte Selver

Part I: Discovering What Is Already There

CHARLOTTE: We have nothing to teach you. We only help you to discover what is already there, inside you. Our method is that there is no method. It is a very sensitive inquiry, a very sensitive discovery which everybody makes for himself through his own experimentation into what we actually become aware of when we begin to use our biological equipment more sensitively, more sensibly. It's not an empty phrase to say, for instance, when something doesn't fit fully into reality that it is non-sense. And this sensing—this possibility of becoming more alerted in our senses, and using them more fully and more altogether—this is the content of our work.

We are all born with our senses

CHARLOTTE: Sensory awareness is something that is quite natural to the human being—or at least it should be quite natural. We are all born with our senses and in the course of our development from earliest babyhood we are exercising the senses without having special instruction in regard to them. Through all the exploration and all the things the baby and little child meets, these senses develop—by themselves. Now it would be wonderful if it would go on like this, but very often in our development certain influences make themselves felt which make the rounded development of our sense perception impossible. Seeing and hearing are the senses which are exceedingly developed, while the ones which have to do with real physical nearness and an uninhibited use of all sensory possibilities (touch, taste, smell, and the kinesthetic sense), are very often very much discouraged. So that we stand before the fact that most adults are not—any more—fully and freely using their senses.

In order to come to a fuller use of senses, the organism has to be in a state of balance, in a state of, let me say, tranquility. At the same time, in a state of reactiveness. So there are two things which are necessary, which in a way seem to contradict themselves: One is the state of quiet, so the impressions can reach us; the other is a state of aliveness, so that impressions can be reactively met.

Now, it happens that in our education we have been constantly admonished. "Pay attention!" "Listen when I talk!" "Look at me when I speak to you!" "Concentrate!" "Make an effort!" And so on. All these demands have brought about an attitude which is very different from the natural and healthy state of sensory reactiveness. By and by the child comes to believe that it has to do something in order to see, in order to hear, to smell, feel, or taste. This tendency to make even tiny efforts disturbs greatly the possibility of really receiving the full amount of sound, or sight, or whatever we get through our sense perception. At the same time it brings us into a state of constant effort, an effort which is completely unnecessary.

Allowing clear, quiet reactivity

CHARLOTTE: We do not think that thoughts come: We have to do the thinking. The more effort we make in thinking the better we think—we think. Through our education's imposed inferiority complex we think we cannot simply function. And this is a very great handicap. We are not used any more to a healthy condition, in which our sense organs function automatically and sharply, without our making an effort. We are not used any more to the quick feeling of potency; we do not allow this brilliant state of clear, quiet reactivity. Instead, we are all the time driving ourselves into the neighborhood of something which would function naturally by itself.

In this seminar you will see how deeply ingrained it is in us, how much we have to work until we come to a healthy use of our sense organs which are there simply to be open. There are two ways we will go. One is coming into a state of sensitive quiet in which sensations can reach us. The other is coming into a state of vitality in which, as a matter of course, our senses become more reactive, and we don't need all this fuss any more. So, I want to go these two ways with you and find out how far we come.

First, I want to mention that we work a great deal with closed eyes, because the sensations of our organism are very different from what we see of our organism. What we feel feels always different from what we see. So it would be good not to try in any way to look. And when we give a vacation to our eyes, let them rest, chances are that the rest of us is more alerted.

A beginning would be to make acquaintance with the busybody in us, the head. I would like us to find out what, if anything at all, we can perceive of this area of our organism where we suppose our head is. I would suggest that we come up to standing. . . .

So, while we are standing I would like you to allow your eyes to gradually close. . . Very nice to feel how it feels with closed eyes. . . . And I would like you to allow your eyelids to lie comfortably and gently over your eyeballs, not to press, not to squeeze, very easily and gently, so that you could gradually permit them to come more to rest. . . .

Then I would like you to feel whether you could gradually give up any tendency of focusing with your eyes, even with closed eyes, . . . to let your eyes actually comfortably rest in your head . . . and feel whether you could give up any intention to see, even with closed eyes. . . .

And then, very gently indeed, I would like you to allow your eyelids to open again like a curtain which gradually opens . . . and feel whether your eyes could gradually be unshielded . . . and whether they could be so that you are not right away picking at something with your eyes—not right away piercing with your eyes, but whether your eyes could be easily and comfortably open without that you focus on anything. . . .

Ja. Would you sit down.

You know, sometimes when you listen to music you close your eyes and you find it very helpful. You do not say, "When I close my eyes I fall asleep." You are fully given to the music, and that's exactly how, right now, that you are simply fully given to let your eyes and eyelids come to a little more rest.

So, as you are sitting, I would like you once more very gently to allow your eyelids to close, and be good neighbors to each other . . . and feel what that does to your eyes themselves. . . . And when you have given up all seeing—which takes a little time, until the activity of seeing is gradually abandoned so that your eyes can easily rest . . . then I would like you also to feel whether it's possible to become a little more restful in your thoughts. . . .

Without jumping at anything at all, just as peaceful as you can be, I would like you feel what, if anything at all, you can become gradually aware of—of sensation of this that you call your head. . . . Is there anything at all physically noticeable in the direction in which you suppose your head is? . . .

As I said before, it's perfectly different from what you might ever have seen, so give up imagining it. Just feel if, when you give time and you don't hurry yourself, what sensations, if any, come to you up in there, above your neck? . . . Don't choose. No matter what it is, how little, how ridiculously little a sensation—no matter whether it feels good or not good—it doesn't make any difference. . . . What do you feel, if anything, in the area where you suppose your head is? . . . Is it possible not to "try to feel," but to allow sensations to come? . . . Make your discoveries in this respect, and then I would like you to allow your eyes to open.

Was there anything? . . . Was there anything at all? Yes?

Student: I'm probably imagining it, but I could swear I felt the curve of what might be the scalp either curving ... or pressing, or something into the top of my back. Is that possible?

Charlotte: Yes.

Student A:[3] What I felt was my right cheek . . . from underneath. It's tingling.

Charlotte: Come as close as you can to what you really felt.

Student A: It's coming from way underneath and it's very, very slight. And there's only the one cheek [*laughs apologetically or nervously*].

Charlotte: Ja. So what else? . . . Yes?

Student: This is the first time I had realized that my ears were where they were [*general laughter*]. That they were—actually had weight. . . . And you could tell that they were there—without having to look.

Charlotte: Yeesss. What else? . . . Yes?

Student: I felt the tingling on top of the scalp ... in a small area ... and also I could feel the heat of the blood in the ear and the slight little ringing.

---

[3] A student who speaks more than once in a session is identified by a letter.

CHARLOTTE: I see. . . . Ja? Yes?

STUDENT: I felt as if my head—the entire cavity—were expanding out so that I didn't feel any boundary or any outline.

CHARLOTTE: Uh-huh. Ja. It's very strange, this sensation of getting wider or so. . . . How about the others? . . . Yes?

STUDENT: I had a sensation across my cheeks, and then up from the back of my neck and around . . . and then inside my mouth. And then my head got so heavy I couldn't hold it up. At the last I felt that there was kind of a bar through my head that went clear up to the top.

CHARLOTTE: Uh-huh. Yes?

STUDENT: I would say the gentle closing of the eyelids gave me a feeling of caressing the whole head. It also gave me the very strong feeling in the ears, that was spoken of before. I was very much aware of my ear, the little part underneath, the soft part.

CHARLOTTE: Uh-huh, yes. Anyone else? Anything else? . . . Yes?

STUDENT: I was only conscious of my jawbone. Not at all of any boundary, just the jawbone. I felt the weight of my head, but at first my eyes just felt like holes; and the mouth had a funny, amorphous feeling—a sort of a burning fullness around the mouth.

CHARLOTTE: Wonderful. I think you are already quite sensitive. So, let us make a little second experiment in this respect. I have to ask you one thing: At first you don't approach it at all. You spend a little time to forget whatever you have been feeling, to forget so you are entirely new for the next attempt. Is this clear? Don't right away ask: "Where are my ears?" [*Laughter.*] First forget it and then when you feel your inner is quiet, then you start to dive into the next exploration, simply letting sensations come as they come—insofar as the presence of this so-much-cherished part of us, the head, is concerned.

Would you close your eyes once more, and feel what is now noticeable in your head, so that you have a clear sense of what you feel now. . . .

And then I would like you to open your eyes again. And I would like you to take your own hands and take your head between them. Often you might have to touch quite firmly, kind of feeling with your hand what you, so to say, meet up with when you are bringing your hand to different parts of your head. . . . And you just stay there and feel what you can feel between your hands. . . . And, at the same time, feel what the touch of your hand creates of sensation inside, and which way it influences you. Is this clear? So you go about it and you stay exactly as long as you need in order to really feel what you have between your hands . . . and also let the touch of your hands influence you. . . .

And when you have done that, then you go to another place and do the same. . . . Now, take your time and give all the possibility of changes which you might need. . . . How does it feel, what I have there between my hands? . . . And do my hands influence me inside? . . . Be sure to have the patience to stay until you feel also that the effects of your touch can be permitted inside the head, how it influences you.

And then you go somewhere else. Go gently, approach your head feelingly. . . . You might touch your eyes, go anywhere. . . . Let the hands go down before your arms are tired, and come up again as soon as you can. . . . It needs a strong touch in order to influence the inner enough so that the inside of our heads can feel our hands and can react to the touch, so give yourself time for it. . . . Feel the full hand. Palms are very important, fingertips, the fingers, all the long length, so that you really can have contact, fully. . . .

When you leave, please continue to be sensitive . . . and leave your eyes closed. . . . So, I would like you to very gently leave the head now, all of you, and just take a little time and feel what you feel now of what you call your head. . . . Is it the same as it was before you started this touching, or has it changed? . . .

Now I would like you to sit down on the floor and pull your chair in front of you. Turn the chair so you can support yourself with your elbows on the seat. And once more touch your head with your hands. Stay there comfortably for awhile, and just feel how the touch gradually influences you inside the head. . . . Then you can go with your hands to another place, turning your head and changing with your hands, and very thoroughly and firmly try to influence your head—quietly and fully—with the touch of your hand. Be interested in what you get aware of as you are doing this. Under your hand you wake up more—insidely, a soothing effect, insidely. . . . With all this, use the full friendliness and good touch of your hand, every touch being new to you so that you can respond to it all through the head. . . . Let every angle from which you touch your head be new to your hand so that you can feel what you have between your hands, and without that you in any way disturb the attitude of being there for something. . . . Give time for the touch, being permissive. . . .

I would like you to very gently go away from your head with your hands, and still sitting, without opening your eyes, feel again what comes now to your attention in the area of your head. . . .

And then I would like you to come up and sit down on the chair. . . . Whose sensations have radically changed? . . . Yes? What was first and what was later?

STUDENT: The finding of an objective feeling. First as if it were someone else's head and as if someone else's hand were touching my head. . . . I lost my subjectivity. When I took my hands away I had a very light feeling of the bone structure as though the bone had disappeared and it were light. . . . And I didn't have much sensation the first time.

CHARLOTTE: Yes. . . . How was it with you?

STUDENT: Well, the first time it was an image of my head and my brains. But later, when I had approached it several times, I began to feel it more as sensations. And when I took my hands away, my head felt at ease [*laughs*]. Naturally, the way a head should feel.

CHARLOTTE: Yes. Anybody else anything very astonishing? . . . Yes?

STUDENT: My head felt much softer than I thought it was going to feel. Something like a baby's head, softer than I thought it was—instead of hard and bony.

STUDENT B: It was interesting to me that there was one spot that was awful, as if there was something coming out, coming out and making a round, like a goose bump.

CHARLOTTE: Yes, it is very interesting: Often the contour, everything, changes. Was it disagreeable?

STUDENT B: Yes, but I couldn't avoid it.

CHARLOTTE: Yes. Anybody else anything? Who has no head any more? Who felt nothing anymore?

STUDENT C: My sensations were in the bone structure. My head seemed quite vacant inside. I didn't realize it was vacant [*loud laughter*].

STUDENT: I felt ownership of my head for the first time. It was very different than before.

STUDENT: I felt so much more. I felt much kinder toward myself after the experiment.

STUDENT C: The second time, concentrating on my head, it felt almost like a balloon—very light, but as though it were held up. There was heaviness here in the neck. Were my head not anchored here it would go floating off. In touching the head I just felt bone. That was all, nothing new. Oh, I felt stimulation.

CHARLOTTE: It did stimulate you? You felt it influenced you somehow inside?

STUDENT C: Yes, the stimulation. Then a slight pressure here, when I took my hands away. It was not quite pleasant, but not disagreeable.

STUDENT: My head felt very light when I held it. But the harder I pressed, the more it became compressed; and I felt I could just squeeze my head to nothing. It kept getting smaller and smaller. And when I took my hands away it felt just WONDERFUL—so light and airy and relaxed.

CHARLOTTE: Yes. . . . Now I think we have to go on to one more thing. This time I would like you to come up to standing.

Take your fingertips and lightly—or stronger, according to what you need and what you like—you begin to tap your head from all sides, to stimulate it really and fully. . . .

So you will find while you are doing it that you need here lighter tapping or stronger tapping. You may need to stay somewhere longer in order to get really as much stimulation as you need. You have to come back here or there, and so on. . . . So you tap to the heart's desire, and adjust the tapping exactly to what you need. Tap your skull and tap your face everywhere as vigorously or as lightly as you feel it's good for you. . . .

Feel whether with the tapping you could kind of aim at the inner of the head, at the brain tissue, and at the whole interior of the head, so that it isn't only that you tap your skin and your skull but it can go on. . . .

Now stop. Leave your eyes closed, and take a little time to feel what this tapping does to you still afterward—what it begins to create in you. . . . Let stimulation go on through you wherever it wants to go, wherever it wants to spread to. . . . How does it introduce itself to you now? . . .

Once more, please serve yourself exactly as you need it, and refresh yourself and stimulate yourself in a most delightful way. . . . Is it possible to let this tapping in? Not to push your head against it, not to look out towards it for anything, but to be entirely receptive to the tapping through the whole organism? . . . And lightly, so that your fingers are like staccato, that you are not too heavy on yourself. . . . It's very much, when you tap, that you feel that it's not just the one facade, not one side or the other, but that you are influencing yourself throughout. . . .

Feel from place to place and refresh yourself everywhere, including your cheeks, your jaws, your mouth, your nose, everywhere. And feel whether you can be as permissive as possible to this stimulation to right away sink in, go through, and do what it wants to. . . .

Please stop again, and without opening your eyes give time for the absorption of what you have been offered—what it brings about. . . . You are digesting it. . . . The whole organism is willing to take it up. . . . Feel what is now.

Not what you do, but how you do it

CHARLOTTE: Living has nothing to do with methods. We learn from ourselves, or the seagulls, or from little children, or from growing plants, what living means. And in this way we learn something that comes directly from nature—rather than what is in textbooks and is advertised as 'the new techniques'. There is something very sacred about our nature and the nature of things—the nature of coming together, being together, getting in contact with each other and having sensitive connection to what we are doing—which has nothing to do with techniques. The more you forget them the better. The less you are reminded of what you learned as to 'how it is done' the better. For instance, I have never an idea of what is going to happen. I also have no idea how I will work with you at the next moment. I wait until it becomes acute and kind of feel my way through to what will be necessary next.

The very basis of the work, the very core of the work, is that everything we do can come always anew, . . . always sensitively anew, to be discovered and realized. Discoveries can happen anywhere. It doesn't make any difference what you do. The question is not what you do, but how you do it. When you come closer to how it is to walk, for instance, how it feels, what it opens up in you, what actually happens—then you can suddenly feel, "My God, it's all there! Thank you!" You become grateful. That's a very, very different thing from the usual way of being taught: "Now, do it right; do it the way I show you." What's right? Instead, you feel how it wants to be done—in you at this moment—and you follow your own feeling. And that's it.

Willing to become more originally ourselves

CHARLOTTE: Whether we admit it or not, only we can feel best what we need. When we care enough—when we do not think, "Oh, it's only me!"—we will come to this discovery. Who knows this kind of thing? "It's only me!" Be sure not to fall into this trap. Because each one of us belongs to everybody, . . . and everybody and everything belongs to us. We are part of the whole, and as part of the whole we are just as precious as anything else is precious. Realize that every breath in you and every drop of blood in you is the same life substance as in everybody else, and it's just as important and precious as that of everybody else.

Biologically we are the same, but we each have our own history and are different. . . . So, we have to have respect for our own way, as it wants to happen in us now, rather than try to imitate other people's way. It needs a little more courage, you know, a little more willingness to become more originally ourselves, rather than to be a duplication of others' thoughts and expectations.

There is another point which I would like to make. In this work we are not interested in achievements or that things get 'better'. We do not try to 'cure' people or make them 'better'. When a person begins to really unfold, you know, he develops quite naturally. He doesn't have to try to develop. It comes by itself. So the whole work is, so to say, finding out what happens in going through certain experiments, what insights— what new necessities—come in us. It is important that you realize that this is not 'exercises'. And also it is not a therapy. It's something in which a person finds his own availability for what he is doing. Please remember, I'm not a therapist. I'm just—I may say—a by-sitter. I am sitting by while you are discovering things. All I can do is ask a question or give you a task in which you recognize certain things. I do this because I esteem you.

Finding out for yourself

CHARLOTTE: I don't want to take away from you your discoveries. I don't want to give you pre-chewed knowledge. I think you have enough of that. You have to get going yourself. One thing you probably have noticed—not only in what we say but in what we do in class: that the emphasis is on finding out for yourself. Not saying, "This is right," and "This is wrong," you know. Not giving instruction as to how to accomplish something, but giving the person an occasion to find out for himself. This is very basic in our work! Giving the honor to the person to explore, and not to teach him how things 'ought' to be.

In ballet, for instance, you learn and learn, you exercise and exercise, you force yourself through all kinds of positions to fulfill the ideas of ballet. Only a few great dancers have overcome this training. They go beyond it. Everybody else gets stuck in it. In our work we feel that mechanical exercises endanger the development of a person because when one follows such exercises sooner or later one gets stale. This happens when one approaches things in a 'trained' way instead of letting things develop in their own way.

As a young woman I was very much trained. I had my diploma from the Bode School as a teacher of rhythms—dance-like rhythms, you know—and when I came for the first time to Elsa Gindler they were working on jumping. I had been jumping all the time in the Bode work, but Gindler said to the students, "Do you feel the floor under you from which you want to jump? Have you ever experienced the air through which you jump? Do you feel the space in which you move?" That was entirely new to me. Air? Space? Floor? What are they talking about? So at the end of that session, after seeing what was happening, I was entirely undermined. I had the feeling that what I had been doing was no good for me, and I had to go into this work, . . . because it made so much more sense.

The world as taught and the world as sensed

CHARLOTTE: You know, one is taught certain attitudes, certain motions, and in learning these things—this motion, that motion, so far this direction, so far that direction, and so on—one feels secure, so to say, under this teaching. I had one student who was a famous movie and stage actress. She was sent to me by Erich Fromm, who said, "I simply cannot do anything with her. She is so dependent that she cannot have one thought alone." So she came, and I started to work with her. She said, "With which leg should I start first?" "In which direction should I go?" "How far should I go?" And so on. She would ask me for every tiny little bit, as though I was her director. Because in acting she was used to having the stage director tell her every little thing that she should do. On film I have seen her sliding down a banister and running away, and I was delighted with the way she did it. You know how children do it . . . coming down—ffssssshhh!—and jumping out. And every bit of that was shown her by the director! I tried to work with her, but I must tell you I gave it up. I just couldn't stand it. To be asked every little bit, so that she could completely rely on me, you know? She was, so to say, my trained horse.

If a dancer or an actress, or anybody at all, comes and sees what we are doing, they may think, "This is physical education, this is calisthenics." They may not penetrate into what it actually is, namely, sensitizing a person to the degree that the person can feel whether what he or she is doing really comes from within—or whether it is mechanically learned, is habit.

For those who begin to find out the inner content of this work, it becomes something entirely different. If you are doing ballet, or T'ai Chi, or yoga, or whatever, be sure that you recognize that you are following a set form. Even in that the work can bring you to be more genuine within the form. But when you come here you are looking for something quite different. You are looking to dig into your original nature, if I might say so. To come again into the innocence of movement which young children have, who are so beautifully moveable and so graceful and so real in what they are doing, yet they are not trying in any way to be graceful. Because

12

every movement and every way in which people do things, when they freely function, cannot be different from graceful. But the idea of grace is not there, you know. These people who are moving all the time as though they are standing before a mirror: they have an image of themselves moving, but do not feel their movement.

Yesterday I began to read Alan Watts's autobiography.[4] He makes some very interesting comments, which I would like to read to you. He says, "An enormous amount of philosophy, philology, and even psychology strikes me as a discussion of words and concepts without relation to experience.... There is too little recognition of the vast difference between the world as described"—let me say, *as taught*—"and the world as sensed." And he continues to speak about reality "as seen and felt directly in a silence of words and mindings." That means sensing when everything is quiet inside us. At last he says, "I'm trying to get thinking people"—which we all are—"to be aware of the actual vibrations of life, as they would listen to music." And he ends by saying, "Ideas, beliefs, and symbols are natural expressions of life, but do not, as they so often claim, embrace or explain life."

When Alan Watts first worked with me long ago he exclaimed to me, "But this is the living Zen!" For Zen also tries to find the essential nature in man. It is not going back and becoming just like children, because we have the experience and the consciousness of adults. We have gone through all the conditioning and all that has happened to us, and this we will never forget. The past is, so to say, our property, and it will in a certain way help us to understand what is happening now. So when you find you are repeating yourself, recognizing that you have been doing this in the past and are doing the same again—you can let that go. But you can only let it go when you recognize it as repetition and experience it as such. It's a hard nut. Goethe said, "God created the nuts for us, but He didn't crack them."

We are the ones who have to crack the nuts. And cracking one of them means coming gradually to see that we behave how we have been taught. I am a good girl when I obey Mother, you know? Mother says so and so, and Mother has learned it from Grandmother, and so it goes

---

[4] Alan Watts, *In My Own Way: An Autobiography* (New York: Pantheon, 1972).

on. But in the moment in which I am living for what is genuine I have to recognize what is ungenuine, and that's the cracking of the nut. What we are doing is digging very deep down in us, so that gradually what is ungenuine in us is going away, and by and by we are coming into the neighborhood of what is still alive down there but very feeble—what is really ourselves.

That's the Way, that the Buddhists call Tao, . . . Tao, the Way. And every step into the direction of the Tao—of what is more genuine—is wonderful, when you begin to recognize the difference between habit and a genuine occurrence. At first what we are used to usually seems good just because we are so used to it, but gradually we can recognize it as habit, what we have learned, sitting like a big coat of shellac over us. When we recognize that there is something different, something more genuine than habit, and we turn to the direction of that something different, then every step feels good. Very good.

So every bit which happens in you, in a way, is sacred. You have to acknowledge it, then it may lead from there to something else, . . . or it may not. We don't know. We don't know what can happen before it happens. If that is clear, then you get this kind of inner modesty and respect for your own functioning.

"Forget it!"

CHARLOTTE: The last time we were at Esalen, we wrote on a blackboard in big letters—all capitals—"Forget it." And that included anything which we had worked on. Which reminds me of a story about Suzuki Roshi. He left his walking stick in Los Angeles when he was giving Zazen there, and one of his devoted students thought, "My God! Suzuki Roshi has left his staff!" So she went and brought him his staff, and on this staff were some Chinese characters. This woman was very curious to find out what this writing said, so she asked him, and he told her, "'Whatever you say is not the truth.'" She was terribly worried. She thought he was speaking in some deep way to her. I found out later that in one way that writing meant, "Forget it."

We sometimes have the feeling that we have now found the truth, and it is for that moment true. It is true for that moment. But there is no such thing as 'the truth'. Nor is there anything like 'the good' or 'the bad'—or even 'the breathing' or 'the sitting'. There's only breathing and sitting and that something is true at the moment, but there's no such thing to put on a pedestal and say of it, "This is THE TRUTH." I don't believe in believing. I only believe in exploring a situation and feeling it out very clearly and finding out what it has in it of truth or untruth for me.

We all love to believe. We love to be followers. Everybody can repeat what another person says. That's no difficulty. But to find out for oneself, to really explore something, that's another matter. Gindler told us, "Find out for yourself. That's the only way to learn. What we are working at needs the greatest honesty and the greatest precision." And she told us one time that she had been speaking with a number of famous physicists, and they told her that about eighty percent of all experiments go wrong. Either you don't start at the right time, or the water isn't heated to the temperature that is needed, or two drops of water are too much in the solution, and so on and so on.

So eighty percent of what even the greatest scientists are doing is unsuccessful because of some inexactness, of some neglect. She said, "When we are following an experiment, we have to be ready for it. We have to know what we are doing. We have to go through it and really sense what's happening. We have to give it the time it needs, and we must do it in privacy, alone. And then we have to pick the harvest honestly." So what is important is that you have time to find out by yourself—and for yourself—without that anybody teaches you 'how it is'.

What is 'me'?

STUDENT C: I had a strange and unexpected experience during a recent experiment. When I do a workshop with you I usually pass through certain stages. And I was passing through a stage of resisting everything you said. Having been through that before, I didn't give in to it altogether. And I know now that there's an element of truth in it. So what happened was that at one point I could allow myself to disagree with you about something and still work with you, . . . still be there. I could let go of all those notions about agreement or disagreement. Then I was just there for the touch of my partner.

CHARLOTTE: This is interesting.

STUDENT C: I could enjoy disagreeing with you.

CHARLOTTE: Ja. Now the question is, why disagree in the first place? What is it that makes it disagreeable?

STUDENT C: Um, . . . I'm stubborn, perhaps.

CHARLOTTE: You say you are stubborn. What are you saying with this stubbornness? Your own opinion? Or what?

STUDENT C: No, it's . . . not really on that level. It's more that in this workshop we're encouraged to really be ourselves in the deepest sense. Somebody said to me yesterday, "Working with Charlotte, I have the courage to be myself." Well, sometime perhaps I'll feel real exuberant when we're doing something very quiet, and what I want to do is run around and holler . . . or tell jokes when everybody's being very serious and reverent. It's more like learning how to neither compromise myself nor to disrupt the class. That's really what I'm calling 'disagreement'. How . . . to be me, when I want more than one thing at a time.

CHARLOTTE: The question is, what is 'me'? Is 'me' the accumulated habits in which I usually live in this world, or is 'me' something deeper which we haven't reached yet?

STUDENT C: It's both, for me.

CHARLOTTE: Ja, you feel it's both. Do you also have the feeling you can get rid of certain things, and then be simply more yourself, and not two things at once?

STUDENT C: Absolutely.

CHARLOTTE: So that's wonderful! . . . Come, give me your hand! [*There is much laughter in the class.*] Good! Do you understand him? We are all full of that. We are all like him. [*Laughter.*] Anything else?

"I don't have to!"

STUDENT D: This is not criticism, but sometimes it seems to me that we replace other 'shoulds' with the 'should' of "You should be free, you should be open." I mean, sometimes it seems there's no difference between the society 'shoulds' and the me-growing-up 'shoulds'—or the growth-center 'shoulds' They all seem the same.

CHARLOTTE: Ja. The second big thing which was put on the blackboard at the Esalen workshop I mentioned was "I don't have to!" You know, I don't think you would come here if you had the feeling that we are not honest in working with you. Now, there is the possibility that we go deeper into what I call our nature. In this workshop we have very much worked with the connection between our structure and our inner self. When we speak about structure, we don't mean it as something only physical. We mean it as a whole human being. When you really experience fully you feel different as a human being. More secure. More settled, and so on. But that comes only by and by.

For now we work together, and we honor each experiment by attending to it faithfully. When we give ourselves to an experiment, then this experiment is it. Do you understand? No matter how you may object to it, in this moment you would be there for it. You would give it respect, give it a chance to teach you something about yourself. Maybe by and by your objections will dissolve. Ja?

STUDENT D: Actually, what went on is that I felt my objection and was able to feel the element of truth for me in it. And then it wasn't superficial any more. I validated myself at a deep level, and then the objection dissolved. I had been putting myself down for resisting, and so I was double-bound. I was angry at you and myself. And then I stopped doing that and said, "Okay, I object. That's okay."

CHARLOTTE: I can only quote my teacher, Elsa Gindler. She said, "We can make putting ourselves down into a life occupation." Why put yourself down? Why not simply experience what happens here?

STUDENT D: Well, I think what I was stumbling over was what was spoken of in that first report: the awareness-work 'should' of being open, of being there for the moment. And I was feeling guilty that I wasn't.

CHARLOTTE: Just a moment! So you weren't there, and you recognized you weren't. To this recognition you bent.

STUDENT D: Right. Right.

CHARLOTTE: Thank that—you recognized it.

STUDENT D: I became whole again at that point.

CHARLOTTE: And then when you give thanks for recognizing it, you can go directly into what you are doing. Who understands it? Instead of saying, "Oh, I should be such and such—to hell with me," and things like that, simply saying, "Oh, wonderful! I feel something which now I can leave behind me."

Not what should be, but what wants to be

CHARLOTTE: Often people translate 'sensing' into "What's wrong with me?" Not simply into "What do I sense?" and then accept what they find. There's no magic involved: When I accept what I find, and recognize it, I can allow change.

We are on a path. We are going on our way and then we come to a split in the road. This way leads into the question of finding and becoming worried about problems, and that way leads into exploration. In exploration, whatever should offer itself as a problem is just there to be explored and to be gradually evened out, and that evening out, that resolution, comes all by itself when we accept the problem as a part of the way.

It's not what you think 'should' be, but what *is*, that is interesting. When you have the expectation that something 'should' be in such and such a way, you will never learn what your nature wants. You have a very beautiful indicator in yourself, each one of you, which always tends toward more functioning, even if we don't understand how. It very often goes for a while through not more functioning but less functioning. In other words, the process doesn't go in a straight line, it goes only the way we can already permit something, no matter where that leads us.

And when there is a 'no' in you, a barrier, don't try to force through it, but first <u>find out what wants to happen</u> instead. In other words, follow up what happens in you. I say "what happens," not "what you try to create."

Have you ever noticed that sometimes when you felt, "This is it," that a little moment later you felt, "No, it is a little more this way"? You thought you had it all, and then something more comes yet, and so on. That's the development of human nature. . . . How we start doesn't make any difference. When we come on the way we are on the way, and we continue to be on the way probably until we die. Every step which we make, and which we feel, unfolds us further. The question is whether we take the first step.

In my first session with Elsa Gindler I got the feeling that everything I had been doing before was wrong. I had to start entirely new. And I had the feeling from the very first moment that she spoke entirely out of my heart, but it took me over a year to recognize that I was doing something else than what I thought I was doing, so strongly was I conditioned by what I had learned. When you begin to wake up you feel more what is hindering you—what is 'not you', so to say. And only by following your own feeling can you get to what your nature actually wants. In other words, when the potato salad is too sour, how do I know? Because I know how it is when it tastes good.

When I began to study with Elsa Gindler I remember what it meant to me when once we did an experiment with a magnet and a piece of iron. As the iron came gradually into a certain neighborhood of the magnet, we could feel that in the iron there was a CLICK! when all the molecules of the iron became attracted by the magnetism of the magnet. So that even in iron there is this kind of turning toward, . . . being there for the power of what is there to beckon. Now when you would permit in your own self this kind of being available throughout your system—in other words, through you—for what you meet and what you can do, then the invitations which the world gives you can have a very rich harvest. We may do things a thousand times, and yet it hasn't clicked yet. Because if it clicks, something in you changes.

We have this marvelous inner possibility to feel when something really clicks. We also have the feeling when something tastes to our taste. You could say, "It needs a little more salt," and you take the salt and you put it in, and you say, "Yes, now it tastes all right," or, "I've put in too much."

In other words, there is something in us which can give us exact information as to how it wants to be. This is built into every person. We have been thoroughly educated not to listen to it. We are educated to follow that which should be, or ought to be, but not how it wants to be. How-it-wants-to-be follows our own way of orientation. The other way follows our conditioning and education, and since we are from our youth accustomed to "Father or Mother knows better," or, "Teacher knows better," we have been thoroughly deprived of trusting this inner wisdom, which each person has in himself, and follow rather the advice of others. There lies great unused richness in us which we gradually have to dig out and develop. And when you get to it you will be astonished what all comes into the open which you didn't know was there.

There is something in us which knows

CHARLOTTE: One of our students told me once that she went to Suzuki Roshi and said to him, "I have the feeling that I have a pit of snakes in my Inner." And Suzuki Roshi said, "Yes. Look very carefully at those snakes." He didn't say, "Throw them out." He didn't say, "Be ashamed of it." He didn't say to do anything about them. He only said, "Look at them." And he didn't say, "Evaluate them." You don't need any evaluation when you are really at work and fully sensing, because when we are really in what we are doing, feeling it, we cannot be watching or evaluating what it is we do. It goes beyond evaluation. You don't have to evaluate any more because you have it. You are in it. You are in contact with it so fully that you can feel which way it leads you. You know? We don't trust our inner nature enough. There is something in us, deep in us, which knows.

STUDENT E: I hear the phrases "honoring what you want to do" or "what you think you should be doing," but there are times when I feel so intense—or that the work becomes so intense—that it's uncomfortable, and I do not want to go to class. It is either honoring that or feeling that I should come to class, because ultimately I don't know what's going to happen in class, and it probably could be very good for me. There's a question of honoring things, honoring my own desire to escape at particular times, as against the feeling I must continue and work very hard in order to . . . grow.

CHARLOTTE: What do you call feeling "intense?"

STUDENT E: Feeling . . . pressure. Feeling . . . the pressure which is inside. Either feeling it in my neck or head, or feeling vulnerable: very fragile and transparent. And . . . feeling fear that somehow I won't be able to handle what's coming next at a particular time.

CHARLOTTE: When you speak of pressure, do you mean emotional pressure?

STUDENT E: Yes.

CHARLOTTE: I would like to say something about this. Does this pressure have something to do with our work? Or is it something which is personal to you in your life?

STUDENT E: It's something that's personal to me. But the work does open me up to certain feelings that are very personal and that seem at times very difficult to deal with.

CHARLOTTE: Now, we are all living here under particularly agreeable circumstances. We are not in New York City. Monhegan Island is a very beautiful place. Fresh air, beautiful landscape. Actually, it's a vacation time. And in this vacation time you have decided to come to work on sensing. Sensing is primarily a play of perceiving the activity of the sensory nervous system. You perceive maybe how your breathing goes. You perceive the world around you. You perceive certain inner changes in the way in which you function. You come in touch with other people. You learn more through sensing about what it is to come in touch.

Actually, in itself all of it is very delightful activity . . . if it is not mixed with some idea of 'shoulds'. You know, "I should this," or, "I should that." But if it is coming out of a sense of hunger for more feeling, or out of curiosity or longing for more depth, and for dealing with whatever I touch—my friends, my tasks, the landscape, my own inner reactions, and so on—if this hunger, this longing, is there then there could also come in some feeling of "I should have it all immediately, and if I don't have it all immediately I'm no good." How does that sound to you?

STUDENT E: I don't know. I'll look at it some more.

STUDENT F: I've been running a question in me—want to or not—of what is it in me that will not allow me to express or to experience my . . . my natural self? What is it? What is the duality of my experience of myself which seems to be in conflict with—or at least at times dominates—what is natural in me? And what is . . . why is . . . why am I created this way?

CHARLOTTE: You are not created this way.

STUDENT F: Oh, I'm conditioned?

CHARLOTTE: I couldn't tell you that. You have to find it out for yourself. But I do believe that it's . . . eh . . . your ego. You know, you have a great deal of ambition.

STUDENT F: Mmm-hmm.

CHARLOTTE: And you have a great deal of passion. I do feel that the simplicity of just being there for what is happening is not enough for an ambitious person. One who always wants something. You don't know yet how wonderful it is to simply be there for what you are doing.

Every recognition is so beautiful, you know. Every coming-closer is so beautiful as long as I don't have the feeling, "I must always understand. I must always feel it." When I was a student, by and by my ambition did fall away. I remember one time when Heinrich Jacoby was discussing the magnetism of the earth, and he said, "You are a part of the earth, of the mass. You belong to the mass of the earth." I flared up and said, "I'm an individual!" He looked at me, and he said, "For your father, you are his daughter; for the clerk in the post office, you are his customer; for the magnetism of the earth, you belong to the mass of the earth." You know, when he said that it was as though a world opened for me: I didn't have to defend my individualism any more!

So maybe I begin to become ambitious, or I begin to become pressured. This, of course, hinders sensing, which is an inner way of development, of getting finer and more and deeper reactions to things within myself. It hinders it because I feel something is there, either behind me or in me myself, which pressures me to get something as fast as possible and as completely as possible. Have you all not felt that sometimes?

Now, if this happens, I think the only way we can deal with it is to recognize it, and then perhaps when we feel that it is disturbing us, that it's in our way, we probably will be able to let it gradually go. Of course, we are educated this way, you know, that somebody is behind us, pressuring us. And if nobody is behind us who pressures us, then we are behind us and pressure ourselves. I remember that the things which I hated most in my mother I did to myself later on. It takes quite some time to begin to recognize such things, and then one can gradually understand it better and it dissolves more and more.

So, when you spoke just now of how the feeling gets so intense that you can hardly stand it, that would mean that in some way or other you pressure yourself. And you may be able to give that up. Actually the more you are not pressuring yourself, the more unemotionally you go into this work, the better. Emotions come in once in a while, but sensing is not an activity which demands emotionality. Emotions are what we bring in. This is what very often happens when an association comes up with something from the past. Or emotion comes up when we, for instance, feel what is possible between people. We are touched, but it doesn't create pressure. We are moved by it. . . . It doesn't pressure us. It might even enlighten you, you know. But emotions are not actually the area of our work.

Emotional reactions are not sensing

CHARLOTTE: I think that we're often very much pulled into emotion. You know, when I ask, "What do you feel?" I mean what do you sense? That means what do you perceive? not what do you feel emotionally? Who understands the difference? We very often use "feel" for "sense," but they are two very different ways of using ourselves. You say, "I feel sad," "I feel excited," "I feel fear," and so on. In other words, "feeling" is mostly used for emotional reactions, while sensing is something quite different. Sensing is the perception which we gain through our senses, and occupation with sensing needs to begin with an inner quiet which makes this perception possible. I would like to say this very definitely, because otherwise we fall into a confusion: emotional reactions are not sensing.

Very often when we come into the neighborhood of sensing, some reactions come up which do not immediately belong to the sensing. They come up out of our big store of memories and associations and expectations and are very often mistaken for sensing. . . . But they are not sensing. When we go into this realm, we kind of bow before the necessities which sensing brings about. We are very often hindered in this through memories which have no place in what we are doing at the moment, but when these distracting memories gradually vanish, we come then really to our experience. It's no 'must', it's no 'ought'. It just occurs. It's a communion, so to say, with what becomes alive in us, what offers itself to us. In meeting what comes up we are in the midst of reality, you know. We give ourselves to it, and anything which is in the way is noticed and recognized. When what comes up becomes more important than what we are doing, we follow it. The task tells us, step by step, what is needed, and when we follow we become renewed by what we do, by our everyday tasks.

You can be sensitive to what is happening in the world, but that does not mean that you are emotionally involved. Emotional involvement—and also thoughts which come about—happen after you have perceived. When we really, clearly have perceived something, then we can think about it. The clearer and cleaner our perception is, the clearer and cleaner our thinking is—and the truer we can speak of sensing.

Being here now

CHARLOTTE: I would like to make this difference very clear to you—the difference between emotional involvement and perception of functioning. I quote Elsa Gindler, who, when somebody said, "I'm afraid," would say, "This is an S.O.S. that means 'wake up more for what you are doing.'" When you are really participating you have a clearer possibility to perceive what your reaction is. Most of our fears come about because we have not yet fully opened ourselves for what we are meeting. Instead we go back to the attitudes which we had from formerly. This kills much of our possibility to answer what is happening now.

Now, coupled with this sensing is our inner informer. We sense something, and in our core, so to say, we are in connection with what is happening; then we are directed to what is most appropriate for our feelings. We need to be quiet enough so that our expectations and wishes and desires do not come in and destroy the possibility of this inner direction.

The important thing is not to look at the work as a source of emotions but as a source of discovery, a source of exploration of natural activities and happenings when we are living our life, being with others and so on. We study the way one can most naturally come in touch with one's own inner and with other people and with our tasks. We study functioning—in the widest and deepest sense of the word.

STUDENT: I gather from what you've said that Sensory Awareness can open up our senses to all that's around us and in this opening up there are obviously emotions involved but the primary purpose of the work is . . .

CHARLOTTE: To become awake. To recognize emotions but not to create emotions, yes. I don't mean to say it is an activity in which emotions have no place. But very often through the way we are conditioned we are so beset with emotions that the sensing is simply not allowed. We are too busy being occupied with these emotional pressures. When you lie down, for instance, and your thoughts go on and on instead of becoming more quiet you build up pressures in yourself in thinking. And then you cannot really follow the work because you are too pressured. You should feel this out a little bit.

STUDENT: I can remember the second time I worked with you, Charlotte. It was following the death of my mother, and when I came to class the first day, my partner merely placed her hand on the top of my head, and tears came. Each time I was touched on the head I had this experience. I was really baffled by it, and came and asked if you could explain it to me. You didn't give me an answer, and later I was able to remember how my mother would always touch my head in a very loving way, and then I got in touch with my repressed grief over her sudden death. I think I have felt a higher level of emotion here than I've ever experienced in a group of yours before, and I have tried to allow that for myself. At the same time I've wondered whether a repressed level of sadness comes out when we're quiet in an accepting, loving atmosphere such as exists here.

CHARLOTTE: Yes, . . . but you see, a hand was put on your head, and nobody in the whole group—including me—had any idea what this would bring about. The hand was brought on the head in order to find out what happens inside when this is being done. For you, this memory of your mother came out. So the question would be, would you share this with us when it comes up? So that it would not be repressed by continuing to work on something else, but you would simply speak it out. Would that be possible when something like that happens? I'm asking everybody.

Student G : You asked, would it be possible? and the answer is: it depends on whether you're inviting us to do that, or not. I seem in this series of classes to be expressing quite a bit of emotion through tears— more than I can remember experiencing at once in my life—and I have reported it at various times in class. I have felt some criticism from people who feel that this reporting is inappropriate, and that it crowds them, and keeps them from sensing. And I don't know whether what you were just saying before was echoing what I have heard, or are you inviting us?

CHARLOTTE: No, I don't invite you. I explained that sensing is something different than speaking about one's emotions. If we would ask you each time, "Why do you weep?" we would have work on emotions, not work on sensing. I do believe that when you recognize an emotion, and you really feel it deeply and you recognize it, you would be able—if you are interested in sensing—to tell the emotion that comes up in this moment, "I will deal with you later. Right now I am working with sensing." That doesn't mean you chase emotion away. You just recognize it. Feel it. And ask it with all kindness to wait until the proper time to deal with it. That would mean that you would be kind to yourself and not push the emotion away and say "Shut up!" but you would give it time to settle in you and then return to what you have been exploring.

Let me give you an example. A man came to me sent by a psychiatrist. The psychiatrist said, "He has such a bad posture he has to come and work with you." I saw the man in private sessions and he was standing and sitting always with one shoulder higher, pulled up. So one day when we were working, I asked him what he could feel of himself and he said "My right shoulder is so much pushed up." And I said, "How does it really feel to you?" And he said, "It is not finished. Shall I finish it?" I said, "Yes." He said "Then I would do this . . ." and threw up his hand and arm in front of his face. He told me that his father beat him in the face and this was the gesture which he always had used to protect himself. He had stopped holding his hand up but he still held his shoulder up. Now, at the moment when he recognized that, we could have gone deeply into his relationship with his father, but he recognized what he was doing and to what it belonged, and that it was just a remnant of something from very long ago. I asked him, "Do you still need it right now? Do you have to protect yourself right now?" And he said no. So I asked him to deal with this question about his father at some other time and now to come back to the work and sense what actually wanted to happen in him.

He recognized that this memory came from long ago and was still pursuing him—as certain pressures may still be pursuing any of us. They are from long ago. . . . At this moment we don't need them. We are at another phase of our life. We can answer these pressures in being here now, instead of staying with what is creating our emotion. There will always be a time in which you can deal with it later for yourself. When it came very powerfully—as in this man—he just spoke it out. And as he had spoken it out we were able to come to the 'now' again. If it's very clear to you what at the moment creates your emotion you can speak it out and then we can come back to the class. But I feel it is of no use simply just to weep and not speak it out.

STUDENT G: That's interesting. I thought at first you were suggesting that I just weep and shut up [*starts to laugh*]. Okay.

CHARLOTTE: I would say sometimes this would be needed. At another moment something else would be needed. I would not want to make a general rule of it. You know, it's a very subtle work, and the subtleness of the work means that we are really there for it, and we do not go with our associations too much. If we do, we are lost in associations and we can never really discover what we have been setting out to explore.

STUDENT: I remember the week in which you heard that Elsa Gindler had died, and you spoke to the class about this. I know you were very moved by it. You took maybe half an hour of the time of the class talking about Elsa Gindler, and then you went on with the work. You expressed your grief because you were able to do it. I think one of the problems is that many of us are not able to express our grief in that way, and are not able to move it away and then continue with the work . . . with whatever is at hand, whatever is to be explored at the time.

CHARLOTTE: The question is, is it not perhaps better when I go through an experience, when I would stand it? It's a very nice word, to "stand" an experience, you know. Instead of being crushed and not deal with it. It needs a great deal of inner readiness and a deep sense of giving myself to something, when I'm willing to take up with an experience rather than to let myself be overpowered by it.

When somebody was overcome by an emotion so he began to weep—it happened very rarely—Elsa Gindler would take a big blanket and would put the blanket around the person, lead the person into the dressing room, and would say, "Now, weep yourself out. And when you are ready to enter the work again, come in again." It wasn't "Shut up!" at all. It was only that one would have the possibility to really take care of it when it was so overpowering, and then come back when he felt he could start again with the work which we were doing.

Part II: Sensory Awareness Is Becoming More Awake

CHARLOTTE: Awareness is a matter of recognition which comes without that one goes looking for it. The finding out, the exploration which we do in this work, is a kind of inner awakeness which is there without effortful watching. Will you close your eyes.... Now, if I invite you to let your eyes open again, you see. You don't have to make an effort to see, you simply see. You can't prevent it. And when your ears are open you hear. You can't prevent it. It's as simple as that. When our consciousness is not blocked or blurred, we are open for sensations. And the sensations come much more precisely and freshly to us than when we make an effort to watch. Sensory Awareness is simply becoming more awake.

Waking up inside

CHARLOTTE: Sensing means the use of the sensory nervous system, sensory nerves which go all through us, from A to Z, enveloping everything. And those sensory nerves can be asleep, or they can wake up. So that when I speak of sensing, it's a waking up inside us. To be alive means to allow this marvelous natural equipment of ours to come into play. Would you all come up to standing, please.

I would like you to begin to slap yourselves.... Now, when you really feel you are doing it, you say, "I am slapping myself."... Ja.... Stop, please.... And whatever you feel now from what you have been doing, speak it out for yourself so it really comes out.... [Sounds of slapping and students saying, "I'm slapping myself."] ...

What's happening ... after slapping? ... [Students no longer speak out, but there are some sighs and yawns.] *Who still feels the effect of the slapping? ... What's happening now through the slapping? ... Just let it out of your mouth....* [Students speak out again: "That feels better!" "Oooh!" "Aaah!" "You can loosen up more," etc.] ...

So . . . you are going to slap yourself once more, when you feel ready. Then, would you say, "I'm going to slap myself once more." . . . [Long pause as students announce their intentions, and then begin to slap themselves.] *. . . And stop again. . . .*

CHARLOTTE: Ja. Would you come a little closer and sit down. Did you enjoy this?

STUDENT: Parts of it. I didn't say, "I'm going to slap myself," because you said, "when you're really ready," and as soon as I approached being ready, then the thought, "I'm going to say something," immediately took me away from readiness and I could never resolve that. . . . So I slapped away because I like to slap. [*Laughter.*]

STUDENT: Quite the contrary for me. I kept waiting to be fully ready to slap and wondering what that would be like and hearing everybody else slapping and saying that they were ready to slap, and feeling, "Gosh, I'm being left behind!" And all of a sudden I just wanted to slap so much I said, real fast, "I'm ready to slap," and I started to slap myself! [*Laughter.*] Because . . . because . . . because I've always been bored with the slapping routine that we do, and it never meant a thing to me until just now. I slapped myself up and down, and said, when I felt it, "I'm slapping myself!" And I was amazed to discover that I . . . that lots of my body is just wood. There's no feeling there and, well, I don't enjoy slapping there. It's just like slapping on somebody else, you know. Well, no. . . they're more fun. It's like slapping on the wall. But there were some spots that . . . all of a sudden they just glowed, and they talked back. And then my hands and . . . and . . . and the rest of me were talking! It was just great! [*Much loud laughter.*]

CHARLOTTE: It's nice after all these years, isn't it? [*Loud laughter continues.*] I'm trying to approach wholeheartedness. Of course, you could go into the experiment by simply doing what I say. But you could also go into it by really feeling what's happening—have your teeth in it. The important thing is allowing that something which is said can go into you and the response could be simply through your own 'now'. We may not yet know how responsive we can be. When after all the work he has done on slapping, he makes such a statement that when he is slapping himself he feels he is slapping somebody else—and then suddenly it's different! Maybe we can discover how it is when we don't build these walls around ourselves, you know, but really are there for something.

It's interesting that in that moment of trying to speak about it, before he came into it, he stuttered. I was delighted by the stuttering because it showed that it was no pre-formulated merchandise. It was no canned food. And that's what I like to get rid of . . . the canned food. So everybody has the full right to wait until it happens, or when it doesn't happen not to speak. By all means. In other words the experience leads to what we say, so that it comes right from experience to saying. Not just out of our minds, our head. . . . I mean it very deeply when I say that only when you feel you are ready to slap yourself do you say so. No one fabricates it. It arises in him. If it doesn't, please shut up. Very important. This is a question of an exchange, an exchange between experience and words. The experience comes out through the words.

You don't really have to slap to become awake. Only in the earliest stage, I would say, is it necessary constantly to slap oneself in order to become awake. Being awake very often involves becoming more peaceful. If we are too much occupied with thoughts and decisions, we cannot be awake to what happens, or to any change. For instance, when you are working by yourselves before the beginning of class, you might prepare by becoming more quiet. Not in just lying on the floor either. You can become more quiet in walking or standing or sitting or anything, so that the gossip in the head stops by and by. And you will come into a state in which what happens inside you could become more clear to you: air exchange; opening; settling; and I don't know what all. So if you would wait a bit and take your time while you are sensing, you might find that somewhere where you are not yet awake you become awake through simply allowing more alerting there . . . without doing a thing.

Everything always new

CHARLOTTE: I would like to mention a few things before the next experiment. The first one is that we are able to change in every moment. What was a moment ago may be already different. So when you have an experience of any kind, and you notice that your sensations change, accept it. Don't try to hold on to what you feel or don't feel at first. I

31

would like you to keep this clearly in mind. The other thing I would ask you to accept is having no experience.

This can also happen at first. But nothing is also something. And it, too, can change at any moment. So, it would be wonderful if you could come into the work without any expectation that right away something would start.

We are here because we are desirous of getting into deeper sensations, so there must be in us a knowledge that we could go deeper. It is like a yearning in us which can lead us gradually in the direction of fuller participation in what we are doing. So, if you have these two things alive in you—the willingness to change and the acceptance of everything as it comes—and follow them with as much willingness and love as you can, then you would have all you need to work with.

Yesterday a number of you felt there was a difference between knowledge which one has in one's head—which one has intellectually—and knowledge which one has through one's whole organism: That there is a split between intellectual knowledge and organismic knowledge. Today I would like to start working very gradually toward unification of the organismic process which, of course, includes thinking, but doesn't separate thinking from other manifestations of your potential. So, I would like us all to stand.

In standing, first make sure that you have a good feeling of the basis on which you stand, so that you feel you are supported. . . . When you are perfectly sure that you can stand here, then I would like you to gently close your eyelids and find how the world feels when you don't have your eyes open . . . whether you have any sensation of what is around you . . . the air . . . and what is under you . . . and of your own inner world. . . . Whether you can feel yourself as you are standing here. . . . Whether you have any sensation of anything that is going on in you . . . any sign of life. . . .

Can you feel your fingertips? . . . Are they alive? . . . Could you gradually become still more awake in your fingertips? . . .

Do you have any sensations in your heels? . . . How do they touch what is under them? . . . Is it a gentle coming together between your heels and the basis on which you stand—or do you press on the floor? . . . If you press, maybe you could change your weight a little bit. Then the connection to the floor could become a more friendly one. . . .

32

Do you have any sensation of your chest? . . . Of your belly? . . . Could you gradually become a little more awake inside your chest, inside your belly? . . . And could you become more aware of the area of your eyes . . . and, if possible, get more ease in them? . . .

Could you sense what is around you . . . and become more conscious of what is inside you? . . . And allowing all this to continue in you, I would like you to open your eyelids and to feel if it is possible to stay in contact—in sensory contact—with all these aspects of living when your eyes are open. . . .

And then I would like you to lie down for a little while, and continue to just make friends with your own selves, please. . . .

I wonder whether anyone of you could follow these questions, and may have had one or two interesting experiences. Were there moments in which you could feel one of the things I suggested you get in contact with, and other moments in which you could not?

STUDENT: I didn't feel anything until you asked what was the contact of my feet with the floor. I felt that, and I felt that it was heavy. I started shifting my weight so it would feel better and I wouldn't hit the floor with such force. Then I started feeling the other things.

CHARLOTTE: In other words, something which at first was not felt became felt, and you found that, in allowing a little shift in your weight you stood differently. Yes.

STUDENT: I became conscious of the same thing, but found that I couldn't shift my weight due to an old foot injury. After that I became very conscious of how much that affects me all over—I noticed I couldn't relax my eyes; they tensed up because my standing was uneven.

STUDENT: When you talked about the feet on the floor, mine weren't. I don't have my heels on the floor: I'm like standing on my toes, you know, like being ready to run, ready to go someplace, but not putting your foot on the floor real hard—standing more on the toes. So then I stood on my heels and it made my legs feel heavy.

STUDENT: When you mentioned the heels and you said get friendly with the floor, I felt that my heels weren't friendly, so I shifted my weight forward. Then the heels became friendly, but the other part of my foot didn't. So I shifted weight back and forth like rolling and wondered if that would be friendlier.

CHARLOTTE: Maybe. It's at least the first possibility of feeling that you can change. You can change in your sensations, and you can change in your distribution of weight. And each change feels different. It interests me very much what we are all saying about standing.

STUDENT: I had the feeling of being completely out of balance, and all the time I had the tendency to open my eyes and see where I was. I became aware of this, and then I had very good feelings.

CHARLOTTE: Who felt also that having our eyes closed makes us more conscious of the hazards of standing, of the very subtle balance where the slightest little bit of change in weight distribution seems a huge sensation? So that's very interesting. In other words, you must be prepared to come into the unknown space of subtle elasticity in which you become aware that: here it feels better; here it feels pressure; here's ease; here's again more pressure; here it's wonderful, and so on. And so you learn from it.

STUDENT: The first time, when you asked us whether we felt the air and the ground, I was aware of the unknown that was outside me. Then, after we were experiencing our bodies, and we felt the air and ground again—instead of its being unknown and dark, for some reason it was known. There was a very different experience of the outside world, and yet I hadn't done anything but feel myself.

STUDENT: When I was standing I came to near panic because I felt I wasn't getting enough air. I could feel the breeze but I felt like I was suffocating, and I was very uncomfortable in my chest and my belly.

STUDENT: When you asked us to notice our surroundings, I was first thinking, "Ah, I hear the ocean; I feel the breeze." Later I felt more my body in space.

STUDENT: I found it very hard to stand erect in a position that required little effort. It seemed like just slight changes were going to throw my balance off so it was a big effort to hold myself. Hard to find a straight line rooted right to the ground.

CHARLOTTE: Forget the straight line. That's an image. And just allow what you feel. Let yourself be led by your own body to what feels more like standing.

STUDENT: Ever since breakfast I have had a slight case of hiccups. When you mentioned the belly I became very much aware of it. Maybe that's not what you wanted us to be aware of, but it was kind of noisy so that's all I heard. But as soon as you mentioned eyes, I completely forgot about the hiccups. You told us to do different things, but I think the strongest was something with the fingertips. Then I completely forgot everything but my fingertips.

CHARLOTTE: I must congratulate you on your first reactions, and your alertness to what we have been doing. Now I would like us to continue working together. Would you come up to standing.

Each one find a partner. I would like you to face each other. And come close enough so that you can hold hands with each other. So here you are together to support each other with your presence. . . . I would like you to close your eyes and to feel whether, when you are standing in contact with somebody else, you have a clear feeling of standing, . . . whether being in the neighborhood of your partner makes it easier for you to stand securely. . . .

After a little while, go very gently with your hands on the shoulders of your partner, and stay this way together, allowing any moving—a little bit more forward or backward—which you need to have a good contact with your partner. . . . So there you are standing together. . . . Then, very gently, you remove your hands from the shoulders of the other and stand, again, alone. . . . Feel whether you can find a way of standing in which you feel you are really standing. . . .

With your eyelids closed, seek once more the hands of the other person. . . . Feel how this influences your standing. . . . Find your way to the shoulders of the other person . . . . and feel how this little movement of coming from touching hands and coming to touching shoulders, how this feels through your whole organism. . . . Then you'll go gently away from the other with your hands, and feel how standing is now. . . .

I would like you to allow a little sway, going forward and backward on the floor so you will have a very gentle and small change in weight distribution. Allow it very gradually—very little, the less the better. . . .

And while you are allowing this, I would like you to go with your hands gently on top of your head, and let your hands settle up there, and feel whether you can allow this change in weight distribution still smaller and more gentle so that you can hear the grass growing in feeling out how it feels in every one of those tiny little moments of change of weight. . . .

When the weight goes a little bit more to the ball of the foot, and goes a little bit more to the middle, and toward the heels, . . . is there a place where the connection to the floor is most agreeable? And where you have the impression that it feels easiest, you allow a little longer standing, more quiet there. But always staying moveable. . . .

And we once more, in our changing of weight, go very gently, a very little, forward and backward, just to recognize the different possibilities of connections with the base on which you are standing. . . . And then, gradually, become still more quiet in your movements until you land where it feels easiest. . . . Thank you very much. Will you sit down please. . . .

And now will you lie down and go with your feet high in the air. And while you have your feet in the air, please move them any way you like to. . . . Just feel, "What can I do with my feet? . . . with my toes, with my instep, with my arch? . . . What can I do with my ankle joints to feel how moveable, actually, the feet are?" Curl and twist and move and stretch them and bend them. . . . But taste it. . . . Not too fast—so that you can really feel what you are doing. It's saying "good morning" to your feet. . . .

Now I would like you to stroke your feet with your feet. Each foot is, so to say, stroking the other, going around the other and letting the other rub it or stroke it, or embrace it—anything which you feel like permitting. . . . So that you really wake up in your feet. . . . And when you are really good and awake, then both legs come gently down to lying on the floor. . . . Now that you are lying, feel whether you can stay awake in your feet, and your entire self awake toward the feet. . . . Please give occasion for each foot to lie on the floor so that you don't diminish the possibility of letting yourself be alerted toward the feet and in the feet. . . .

Very soon you will be standing again, and I would like you to feel whether you could prepare innerly to be very alerted for standing and afterward in standing. . . . Come up to standing when you are ready. . . . Is there possibly something like a brand-new standing? . . . Who's a little more awake now, I wonder? Ja? So then, let's all stretch! . . .

Would you all jump a little bit—from one foot to the other, please. . . . Each foot saying hello to the floor each time you come down. "Hello! . . . Hello! . . . Hello! . . . Hello!" . . . Be sure your heel is saying something to the floor. And your toes. And the ball of your foot. . . . For the next twenty minutes we are continuing to jump this way, so be prepared! . . . [Much laughter.] . . . Now we are going to say, "Ha!" each time we come down. [Chorus of "ha! ha! ha! ha!"] . . . . Now we say, "Hoo! hoo! hoo! hoo!" [Chorus of "hoo! hoo! hoo! hoo!"] . . . Stop and lie down again. [Laughter.]

I must say that you didn't give as much honor to the floor as you gave to the air. The ha! ha! ha! and the hoo! hoo! hoo! were much more alive than the touch of the floor with your feet. So, while you are now resting, be sure that you allow as much recovery in your feet as you can. . . . Whose heart is beating? Be happy you have one. . . . Whose breathing is a little more animated? Be grateful that you can change. . . . So, would you stand up once more? We'll try once more. This time pick another partner, please, a different one.

One person is jumping, the other claps his hands for the jumping of the other. After the jumper has had enough, he gives the jumping over to his partner, and claps for him. Be sure that your jump is just as wonderful and springy as the clap. First, all clap together so you know the rhythm. [Clapping.] So one is clapping and the other is jumping, until you feel you've had enough jumping, then you give it over to the other. Start! [Clapping and jumping.] . . . . Now let's clap much less loud. [Softer clapping.] And the one who claps is not jumping, is a little bit vibrating with the one who jumps. . . .

Sit down please. . . . Now the question would be whether with your clapping you're inspiring your partner, or boring him. Clapping can be very boring. And your approach to the floor can bore the floor terribly, can hurt the floor terribly, or can be inspiring to the floor so that right away something begins to grow under your feet. I would like you to use your hands for a moment, and clap so that you bore yourself with the clapping. [Apathetic clapping.] Now stop. Do you feel anything? . . . Now be very assertive with this clapping, will you? [Loud, fast clapping.]

So, with this inspiration, I would like this half of the group to come up and jump to the clapping. But as soon as somebody bores you, go and tell that person to be a little more inspiring. [Laughter.] So we can bring a great amount of eager freshness to the people we are inspiring to jump. Now, the orchestra begins. [Clapping.] Too fast! Again! Cherish every moment. Your inner reaction to the motion—who feels it as some revolution inside now? Or is it what's going on in circulation, breathing? Let it happen. Don't suppress it. Enjoy it. . . . Now we are preparing for your great orchestral activity. . . . Again we are getting too fast. Much slower. Let me give you the tempo again . . . . Again. . . . Sit down.

So, there are many ways to contact the floor, and it's up to us to contact it in aliveness and freshness, and each time new—not to make a kind of repetitious activity out of it in which, unfortunately, we just go along as often we do in life, repeating ourselves in relationships. We repeat our relationships with other people because we know them already. "My, word, there's my husband; I know him already."

I have a friend—who is still my friend—who is always saying to me "I know what you mean," before I've hardly opened my mouth. The question would be, is it possible to give that up? So that, instead of knowing what your friend means, or knowing what one touches, knowing what one tastes, there is tasting it anew, seeing the person anew, meeting the floor anew. There is a very important measure you have inside to tell you how long an activity can be permitted sensitively so that each time it's new, and the moment when one become repetitious, mechanical. Stop even before there is a danger of becoming repetitious, because then it's no use any more, then the activity only deflates you, so to say. It doesn't give you an inspiration any more.

So, if you are not too tired, I would like you to come up once more. The group which jumped first will jump again, and the others will clap. . . . The people who are clapping with their hands, although you are not jumping, feel the motion in your standing feet to whatever extent it moves you. Does it help you to judge whether you are getting too fast or too slow—or whether you do justice to the jumping people? . . . Now change: those who have been jumping will clap, and those who have been clapping will jump. . . . Stop doing it as soon as you feel you are getting repetitious. . . .

Now, as the last of this, I would like you all, without clapping, to allow the connection to the floor with the heel—anew. . . . Just make a little jump, hardly more than a vibration. Each time the heel comes new to the floor, very light. . . .

Then you come to standing and feel whether you could allow this gentle touch so that the weight can distribute itself more, instead of being either too much on the heel or too much in the front—so that you are altogether moveable, and the connection to the floor is a gentle one. . . . Will you once more vibrate a little—lightly, very lightly. To prepare, in a way, for coming to standing.

*Now let's stand again, and feel whether we can stay moveable, easy. . . .
How does the floor feel now? . . . Allow your eyelids to be closed. . . .
And if there is any sign of inner mobility without actually making any
movements—perhaps just because you are a little more elastic—enjoy it. . . .
When you happen to become entirely still in standing, enjoy that, too. . . .
And feel whether this connection to the floor could even influence you inside
your head, so that the signs of effort and stiffness can gradually vanish, as
inside the head it becomes more permissive and easy. . . .*

*And then I would like you to take your time to lie down once more and
feel every bit of the lying down when you come to the floor. [A very long
pause.] Would you come to sitting again.*

We have gone through a number of different activities. It might be
interesting for you to exchange the experiences you had during this time:
first in your feeling of how it is when you are in contact with somebody
else—in holding hands, in touching the shoulders of the person—and
then later when you left the connection with the person and stood alone.
Was there anything that you felt clearly?

STUDENT: I have an atrophied leg, and both legs were in spasm
before I touched the other person. Then gradually, as time wore on, I
could almost bear to stand on the floor without pain.

CHARLOTTE: So, the connection helped you to be more easy toward
the floor. Very good.

STUDENT: When my partner took her hands off my shoulders,
I got a chill. And then we stepped away, and then coming closer—we
were moving with this rocking motion, or something going on like it
was a vibration of her weight. Then, even standing still I felt a vibration,
vibration, vibration.

CHARLOTTE: Who felt that, too? Sure. Anybody else, in the first,
quiet part of the experiment?

STUDENT: When I stood alone I felt that I was contracting more
muscles in my legs than I had to—just to stand up. I was getting away
from that, but as soon as I touched the other person, I started to do it
again. And then it stopped.

CHARLOTTE: It's very often so that when you 'pay attention' to
something like standing that you use too much effort to pay this attention
and it contracts your legs. What is it to be awake? Does one have to

concentrate on something, or can one feel anyhow, without trying to give special attention to it? These are very interesting questions which we will gradually come closer to.

STUDENT: I was first trying to think about my legs and then in not thinking about them I just sort of settled into the ground with my feet.

CHARLOTTE: This "not thinking about it" is a good clue.

STUDENT: Having the hands on the head is a very odd sensation for me because my hands feel my hair, and my hair feels the touch, but I don't think of the two as being part of me—it's like somebody else is touching my hair.

STUDENT: I was very aware of the front side of me: It seemed very sensitive and alive as I was facing the other person.

CHARLOTTE: How about the jumping?

STUDENT: In the early stages I felt I was kind of clawing the ground. And after the jumping I felt much easier: I felt more relaxed with the ground.

CHARLOTTE: Who else felt easier on the ground after the jumping?

STUDENT: It did just the opposite with me. Before, I had been standing with my whole foot on the ground, and when I jumped I had the tendency to jump on my toes.

STUDENT: You were talking about the boredom thing, and I felt that in the jumping I kind of alternate between its being a new experience and then getting sort of bored. And I just about realize it's boring, and then I shift into its being new again. It's about half time for each.

CHARLOTTE: You know, very often when we are speaking with somebody, suddenly we lose contact and we just go on talking until we become conscious of, "My goodness, I'm just continuing to move my mouth, but I'm not in what I'm saying." Then suddenly we catch up with the situation and come into it again. It's a very good thing you experienced that.

STUDENT: When you said to watch for the boredom, I watched the faces of the people who were clapping. And when they seemed bored, then the clapping seemed boring to me.

CHARLOTTE: In this clapping and jumping, you can see very much what is going on psychologically in the person. We have learned in school to repeat things. When we are doing something like jumping, which seems to be the same, we are so used to repeating ourselves that we lose the ability for freshness. Actually each jump isn't the same because each time you come to the floor you come new to the floor. You come through the air, you come down to the floor, and you go up in the air again so that all the time it could be new.

When you see little children who, for instance, do something again and again because they are fascinated with it, you see that for hours they are doing 'the same thing', but they are in it, with their whole heart, their whole inner. This is the difference between a still-innocent, still-new approach to something we allow to fascinate us, and the unfortunate, conditioned world in which we live—in which everything has to be constantly 'brand-new'—in order to interest us.

I will offer you here a lot of things again and again and again, and you will gradually, in coming closer to them, feel the newness of them. Intellectually you can say, "Oh, yes, I go into the air and I come down again," while you are doing the most boring business in the world. But when you really feel it, then it changes. Then you give your life an entirely new chance.

The wonders of the organism

CHARLOTTE: The change from being limp or insensitive or whatever to becoming sensitized is one of the wonders of the organism. In the moment in which our sensory attention is aroused, changes happen in us. So that at the moment when one might feel, "I'm pressing here," it might change. When one might feel, "I'm too drowsy here," it might wake up.

We spent many months with Elsa Gindler every day in allowing just that. She would ask, "Is there anything where you suppose your head is? Do you feel anything there?" Or, "Is there anything feelable in the region of your pelvis? Is there anything going on there?" And the question would sink in—without that we go right away to look insidely at the place. We are just there and we hear it. That means all our molecules hear it. And then something begins to make itself on its way. That's the riddle. That's the mystery. That's the possibility which everybody has. That's, in other words, sensing.

Now, when you have been jumping, I ask, "Can you feel how the impact of what you have been doing continues in you? In which way it continues, and what happened? Who noticed that I didn't ask you if the impact of your jumping continues in your arms or your legs or your other parts, but in you?

So what you are doing might influence you everywhere—not just where you do it. When something opens somewhere, the need for opening in another area may be strong enough so that it also opens. If we are only sensitive in one area we could eternally work on opening here, opening there, opening another place. When I'm concentrated on one region instead of being both sensitized and changeable everywhere, the hunger for more freedom where it isn't free is augmented very much. (I like to say that when one child gets an apple the other children want also to get an apple, and they begin to complain when they don't get one.) But in the moment in which permissiveness is allowed everywhere we feel something of the self-adjustment of the organism which we hinder when we are too much concentrated on one spot.

This whole question is very much bound with wishful thinking. You know, very often after we have felt an astonishing change, our imagination becomes active, and we begin to feel—to think we feel—reactions. We get our hopes up for more. "How is it here?" we ask ourselves. "How is it there?" When one isn't quite innocent any more, when the sensations don't come by surprise, somehow watching comes in, wishes come in, and we distract ourselves with wanting more than nature offers us at that moment.

Now the art is not to watch it. Not to try to feel it but just to be there in it. You can't be in a higher state of being than to be there for something. In other words you are not thinking about it, you are not watching it. You don't even make an effort to feel it because every one of these things will diminish your possibility to sense, to get impressions.

Most of us are still under the influence of an education in which we were constantly watched, and watching, and judging was constantly asked from us. It was asked by our parents, and it was asked by our teachers, but they didn't understand what the organism actually is. We have very much more endowment for being aware, for being alert, than most people realize. I must admit it is not easy to know the difference between letting something be conscious and watching it. And it doesn't come by trying to get it. It will only come if we are hungry for it. We don't need to watch; we simply could be awake. The moment we watch ourselves, we split ourselves in two.

There is no split between mind and body

CHARLOTTE: Another split became acute yesterday when somebody said "I felt it through my whole body." Who is 'I' and who is 'the body'? I am raising this question. Could you show me where 'I' is and where 'the body' is? [*To a student:*] Could you show me where you are? [*Laughter as student indicates his head.*] Do you agree with him? [*More laughter.*] As one of my students once remarked, "My body is only there to carry my brains from place to place!"

There is no split by nature between this [*indicating her head*] and the rest of us. It's only man-made, this idea of 'mind' and 'body' where the mind is something free-floating and has nothing to do with the rest of us. But in reality it isn't so. This is what Fritz Perls experienced when he studied with me, and has put it down in his much quoted statement, "We don't have an organism; we are the organism." There is nothing else but the organism. Every thought, every intuition, every memory, everything which ever could happen through you comes by the capacities of the living organism. That means of you. If we would begin to experience that what we call 'organism' is living self—from head to foot, including everything—then we would begin to really live and understand. Before that you split yourself.

So the question would be: Is there a state possible in which we can be without watching and without judging, . . . simply awake? Is there a state of awareness possible that is permitted through our whole self from head to foot? So that everywhere we can be aware? You can imagine how much more powerful this kind of awareness would be than when our poor head is so overburdened all the time . . . while the rest of us is just vegetating around, and all this marvelous equipment which we have is restricted or dull, not really helping us to live our lives. So we have to

43

approach the question: could we give up the overactivity in the head and allow fuller living and responding throughout ourselves?

The giving up of thoughts

CHARLOTTE: After this perhaps aggressive way with which I started today, let us all lie down for a moment and please forget what I said. . . .

Allow resting. . . . Rest means something. It means to allow refreshment, to give up working and open up for refreshment. . . . A change from working to permissiveness to refreshment is a very interesting change. For instance, in our limbs we might still have traces of action, or holding, or working. . . . Then it's a difference whether you simply let go—let yourself go slack—or you allow refreshment in your limbs. Allow a change in condition, in other words. . . .

Resting is a great opportunity to become new while we are lying . . . inside our trunk, all through . . . and in our head, allowing more and more permissiveness in giving up effort and allowing there a fuller possibility of change toward rest. . . . So that also in our head we could become gradually more and more refreshed. . . .

Who is still thinking? . . .

Ja, would you sit up, please.

Now, many people have learned to say to themselves, "Stop thinking," and then they control their thoughts and try to stop their thinking. Like somebody who is being choked, thoughts are being choked off. But has anybody noticed that we are sometimes very desirous to come to quiet? That this state of quiet is something wonderful? Quiet is not dullness. It has nothing to do with dullness. Quiet is also not forbidding thoughts. Quiet is a different state into which we gradually can come. You cannot stop thinking from one moment to the other without violating your thinking, but you can—when you feel you would like to rest—gradually allow the giving up of thoughts . . . let me call it allowing peace inside of us. Who can understand that? So it's not a command with the expectation that right away something will happen. It may be a long way which we have to go until we can gradually allow—altogether—more quiet and more resting.

So, I would like you all to close your eyes, as you are sitting.

Feel the actual condition in your head. . . . Be very honest about it! . . . What do you feel there? . . . Is there at all anything in this area where you believe your head is? Do you feel anything there? . . .

If you feel nothing, it's just as well as if you feel something. . . . But if you feel something, what do you feel? . . . Who feels something there? . . . Who feels nothing there? . . .

Thank you very much. Will you open your eyes. . . . What did you feel, may I ask? . . .

Student: I found pressure right here in my temples . . . . some tension in my eyes, and I could feel it continuing upwards. I could feel the whole muscle that goes around my eyes.

Charlotte: Mmm-hmm. How about the others? What did you feel?

Student G: I had a slight headache.

Charlotte: Does the headache say something? Is it from being overused, or is it just an ache? Can you feel what it says?

Student G: It says I got to bed too late last night and up too early this morning.

Charlotte (laughing): Aha! Very understandable. Anyone else?

Student: I felt a heaviness, and a thickness, like my head was just a solid mass.

Charlotte: Aha. Yes. Who can feel with her? When anyone has a similar sensation, raise your land or nod so that we know who has similar experiences.

Student: I felt a heaviness at first, and then as it went on I felt sort of almost a surging, sizzling feeling of warmth, sort of a pulse. Not quite a pulsation, more just a flow.

Charlotte: So, with him it was not just one sensation. It changed. Who felt in this short time also some change in the head? Yes?

Student: Well, I was conscious of nerves and muscles around the eyes which kept constantly changing, . . . tightening and loosening and going in different directions.

Student: I felt my face and my skull, but as though whatever was inside—if anything—was just resting. Maybe nothing there.

Charlotte: Mmm-hmm. With you, too? Aha. You, too, yes? So we have already quite a menu of different sensations. Who realizes that when one really senses, one doesn't sense the same as what one sees? That sensing is something different from seeing? In other words, we would have to give up the images in our head—what we have been looking at in the mirror this morning—and feel, very honestly, simply what is there ... if anything at all.

This is a very delicate subject. We can only very gradually learn to come more into the neighborhood of permitting life. But I wonder who of you felt that in order to come to more life you had to give up the effort of watching? When I make an effort where it's not necessary, I hinder life. Also, if we are receptive inside us there is no room for distracting thoughts. But that doesn't mean that we are dull or sleepy. On the contrary, it means that we are highly occupied with something.

A tendency today is toward meditation, which is based on inner quiet, on really getting rid of this overdoing of the mind and its being busy with all kinds of things, you know? Many people are busy in order to distract themselves from the essential. The question is, how long this attracts you. How long do you like to be distracted? When do you feel, "I'm fed up with that. Now I want to stop and taste this 'really living in the moment'. And give myself to the moment, to what is acute now. When will I be ready to permit that?"

There is a connection here with Zen Buddhism. My own feeling is that what Sensory Awareness and Zen have in common is that we both give the opportunity for our being fully there for what we are doing at the moment. That's what Zen people learn through sitting, that's what they practice in all the different activities with which they are occupied all day long. To be fully there for what one is doing. And if we are fully there for what we are doing we have no pains, or we do not experience them in the same way

Something in us can teach us

CHARLOTTE: There, maybe I am coming to what actually is in my heart. I must tell you frankly that I am not so interested in whether you sit without pains or with pains. What this work means to me is that the person comes to his own nature. And what has been so fascinating to me is the discovery of the magnificent wisdom of the organism: that there is something in us which can teach us constantly how to go about things; that we are able to feel when something is not functioning, and how it wants to be when it would be functioning; and that we can learn to follow it. In other words, what has interested me in this work is the discovery of the creative forces in us, of the possibility of being informed from within how it wants to be, and becoming gradually able to follow that.

In Zen they say, "Buddha is in everybody." That's not a shallow statement. It means something. Buddha is in everybody. Buddha is in you and in you and in you and in you. Buddha is in all of us. That means something in us knows. Something in us can teach us. Something in us can inform us how it wants to be. So that we can feel whether we are coming in touch with another person in such a way that we can be open for the other person, or whether we are not open for the other. We can feel whether we speak the truth or whether we go a little off the truth. We can feel whether we are putting pressure on something or whether we only give our weight to it. We can feel whether we allow our breathing to function as it wants to function or whether we manipulate it. We can feel whether we are dealing with a person and letting the person have his own way of being or whether we manipulate him. And so on and so on. In other words we have the ability within ourselves—if we become more awake—to feel more clearly what our own nature has to tell us. That's the thing that interests me.

For instance, when someone has not been able to sit, and he would give himself entirely to the question, "What does breathing want from my sitting? How do I have to sit so that breathing has it easy to function in me?" The breathing can teach him how to sit. Not what I teach you of breathing, or the Roshi teaches you of breathing, but your own breathing can teach you how to sit.[5] And it can teach you how to run. And it can teach you how to dance. And it can teach you how to make love. And it can teach you anything in the world. In other words, the source of information is really in you. But it's often sleeping. Sensing is to wake up

---

[5] See *Appendix A* for an experiment in being breathed.

for this possibility of really coming in touch with our inner informer, so to say.

It seems so much physical, what we are doing. It isn't. It's just to wake up. When you say you have been working on your legs, you haven't been working on your legs. You have only worked on your waking up. Or let's say you have been working on your pelvis. I heard this in class the other day: "Since we have been working on my pelvis I can sit better." You haven't been working on your pelvis. You have just been waking up more for the possibilities you have. Does that make sense to you? You are not working on your body. You are just working on your getting more awake. And when you get more awake you will notice where you make nonsense. Non sense. You can then gradually from this 'nonsense' come to sense, you know.

In sitting, for example, you have these wonderful hip joints. This joint has a round bone and a pan. And the bone goes into the pan and can move in every direction: up, down, inside, outside, anything. Now, there are some ligaments around this which connect these bones with some other bones. These ligaments can be taut, they can be holding. And there are muscles. These muscles are there to be elastic, to give. And they're also there to hold in moments of danger. But many people are all the time doing as if they're in danger. They hold these muscles so strongly that no movement is possible. When one starts to sit down one has to be moveable. That means one has to wake up in all those tissues that have to do with allowing this moveability. As long as you don't wake up in your tissues you can't get moveable. When you wake up more in them you will find out what all is possible.

So, if you will allow me to say so, this work is a very spiritual work. It has to do with waking up, with getting spirited to the last molecule. Spirited. Because it sits everywhere in us, everywhere.

Allowing the full-fledged permissiveness to sensitivity

CHARLOTTE: Now, when we are on the way to going deeper than we have been going, and to realizing more what we have wanted to realize, we meet also very many obstacles. And many of us let the obstacles defeat our going deeper. We lose interest. We get discouraged. The experience of awakening is not always agreeable. Who has noticed that when one feels more, one feels more in all ways? One cannot choose what one feels. So that it could be that we become much more conscious of certain things that we have till now simply swallowed, or shut off. For such recognition we should be very grateful, because then something new can start.

What is sensitivity, really? It's the admittance of life, of the life of the senses, of which so many people are so afraid. I am inviting you to allow your interior sense, to feel what you feel. And not to shut it off or diminish it, but to really allow the full-fledged permissiveness to sensitivity. When we cut ourselves all the time to pieces, saying "This is good and that is bad," we close ourselves so much off to real, natural experience. This work we are doing may bring you to feel how wonderful, pure, and, I would say, sacred every bit of experience is. You don't have to reject one thing and prefer another.

Elsa Gindler used to say, "When you want to get rid of your bulging stomach you first must have the courage to feel it." In other words, it's very, very important to get more conscious of what is. Then changes can be allowed to happen, so that one can come into the direction that "what is" wants to go. But you have to start being more sensitive for it—immediately. Because otherwise we delay it and delay it and delay it. We like to think, "I will allow it when I get riper for it, when I do more work on it." But this time will never come unless we allow the first step and the following steps.

It is a process into which we invite you. And this process must have its own pace and its own way. Sometimes one draws back from it in order to wait, and then one goes on with it. Sometimes it brings one a little forward, and to the side, and comes back again. It doesn't always go the straight way, so we have to allow it to go as it comes about.

When we showed you our slide lecture—which I have seen about a thousand times!—I was struck by how clearly once again many questions which concern us come out through the pictures. There was the baby sitting on the bench. There was a back on this bench, but the baby was sitting smack on the bench and disregarded the back fully, just sitting like a Buddha. There was nothing, but nothing, which was lacking. . . .He was freely sitting like a Buddha.

Do you remember the group of children? One little child was reporting something to all of them, so there were other little Buddhas sitting there, all ears. Nothing in them was not with it. The little girl that was speaking was speaking, so to say, her heart out. Do you remember her expression? And every one of the children was listening. The little hands and the little backs and the little heads and the little everything, you could feel the listening all through. They were there . . nothing lacking. And you saw them, and I was happy that it brought such great applause.

When you are not yourself any more

CHARLOTTE: And you saw the picture of the pretty girls which we cut out of the magazine, one talking, the other acting as though she was interested, everything very pleasing . . . perfectly false.

So we see what we actually are by nature in those pictures of the children, and side by side we can see what we are being educated to be by society or the advertising agencies, as in the picture of the pretty girls . . . and also in those pictures of the slender woman who was always in a pose, who was always sharply thinking "How shall I do it?" and always creating a show of herself.

And then the man who was sitting entirely exhausted. I must tell you that he is a very good tennis player and a very good swimmer, but he had been training the way runners are often trained, to make a terrific effort. You remember Paavo Nurmi, the great Finnish runner? As a child he ran through the woods to bring his father's luncheon every day. His father was a woodcutter. And Nurmi ran through the woods, and sometimes he saw a deer running, and he ran like the deer. Nobody taught him to run. He just ran because it was necessary and because he liked it. So he became the greatest runner. What we are looking for is what the deer in the woods does.

We have been taught that everything which we learn should be taught to us. We should have teachers for it. These teachers give you one or the other technique or method, and you follow it. For instance, in the success school you learn how to step, how to smile, how to lift a cup. Everything is perfect. But you go more and more away from yourself. You are not yourself any more. You are a circus horse of a certain method of a certain teacher who offered a certain technique which you follow, but it doesn't go really under your skin because you are different from the teacher. Your inner is different. But little children believe their parents. And big adults believe their teachers, and they get all these strange things put over them.

For instance, in Germany one shakes hands when one is a good girl. But when I was a little girl I didn't like to shake hands. My mother would say, "Would you shake hands with Aunt Betty," and I would say, "My hands are dirty," and put them in back of me. My mother would persuade me, and I would take my hands (which weren't dirty) away from my back; but when my mother said, "Now give your hand to Aunt Betty," I would give my left hand. And my mother would be upset. She would say, "Why don't you give Aunt Betty your beautiful little right hand, the nice hand?" So I obliged. I gave the nice hand. And in this way education spoils us. We get something over us which isn't we, and then our teachers reinforce it and we come gradually further and further away from ourselves.

Arriving by following one's own nature

CHARLOTTE: But we have the possibility to come back to ourselves— if we come into real contact with what we are doing—if we arrive, if we are there for it. Yesterday we were working on sitting. I wished I had a film of it. You were hanging, collapsing, flopping on the chairs. All kinds of things. Hardly anybody was sitting. What I have against it is that you call it sitting. That you do call it sitting shows that you are not in deep contact with what you are doing. Then a very strange thing comes about . . . namely, that one never arrives anywhere. One is always either not yet there or is too fast and has gone on somewhere else. One never arrives where one thinks to arrive. That's why in Zen one of the great masters wrote this big news: "Sitting is sitting!"

The little five- or six-month-old Buddha in our picture knew what sitting was. He didn't get educated anywhere. He just followed his own nature, which was not yet spoiled, and on account of that he came to sitting without doubting. And his back didn't hurt. It doesn't hurt when you are sitting.

I see all this friendly massaging nowadays, everybody doing it to his neighbor . . . taking the shoulders and massaging them, going along the back, stroking here, patting there. That this is necessary shows only that we have not arrived at what we think we do. A person who sits has no backache, has no tight shoulders. As long as he still has those he has not yet arrived at the balance and the freedom one has when one is sitting. In the moment in which this is reached, that one arrives where one wants to come, everything is bliss. One feels good in it, and that's one of the signs that one sits, or that one says the truth, or that one is loving, or that one is doing a task to the end.

When we have been struggling with a task for many years, and at last we have fulfilled it, it feels good. Who knows this feeling? Having finished a letter in which one has said what one wants to say, that feels good. Having cleaned the house and it looks good, one feels good. Having spoken in a conversation with someone against whom one has been fighting for a long time, and really coming to an understanding; it feels good.

In other words, what we carry around in what we call our body, and what makes us difficulties like strains and pains is only unfinished business. We haven't arrived. We haven't come to a solution. We haven't digested something, which, on account of that, is half frustrating us. Even when we don't allow the unfinished business to come into our consciousness, our inner informer, which tells us always, "This way, please," is not satisfied, and we feel it all the time saying to us, "Come! Come to the end of it! Allow it fully!"

This is what we sometimes call conscience. I would think we could better call it more refined consciousness. Fuller inner awareness. And most of all the willingness to listen to this constant call which we have in our inner which needs to be satisfied. I think that part of this is behind the great revolution of the students in the sixties who simply didn't want to be anymore in the straitjacket of wrong education. But very often they said No! to everything—instead of only to that which really went against their nature. They had arrived at last at a state in which one simply says No! to everything, whether or not it is genuine.

Take those girls in the advertisement. Suppose somebody has been educated like them—to keep smiling, to be always dainty and nice. Now that's being successful! Today when somebody is smiling one doesn't even look whether the smile is genuine or not genuine. "At least he doesn't make complications!" So we conform with society, we keep smiling, we are friendly, we want to please. We have learned that from childhood on. Please mother. When mother is pleased you get the reward. When mother is not pleased you get punished. So we keep on trying to please.

I've seen many adults who are only trying to please people, to flatter people in order to get what they want. If a person is honest enough to allow himself to feel this, he may find that under this trying to please is a great rage, that he's really deeply angry. But he covers it up with trying to please in order to reach his aim. When he's honest he finds out what actually makes him so enraged, and what makes him try to cover this up with his pleasing attitude. He probably will find out that most of that anger belongs to the past.

Now, you could spend your whole life finding out what happened to make you angry, way back then. But, another possibility would be to realize that your behavior at this moment does not fit what is happening right now—that you are not listening, not feeling it out. When you are truly listening, you are immediately here. You are here for what you happen to do right now. You have your whole being free to be here for it.

Being all there for whatever you happen to do

CHARLOTTE: Charles and I have a workshop which we call "Being All There." That is what you saw with the little children. They were all there for what they were doing. None of them had trouble with sitting. Nobody had trouble with turning his head. Nobody had to be massaged on his shoulders. They were simply there, freely there, and everything that happened massaged them innerly through, and renewed them. That's how functioning is when we function throughout.

In other words the question would be: is it possible that we could feel more deeply and fully what we happen to do at the moment, and allow a fuller contact with it, so that not the past and not the future and not the anger about what happened two minutes ago or ten years ago stands in our way and holds us back—but we are all there for what we happen to do now?

Part III: Letting Ourselves Be Free

Hindering our own freedom

CHARLOTTE: When I first came to Elsa Gindler and lay down in her class, I got strong pains in my legs. And when I got up I had terrible pains in standing, so I went from one leg to the other. I must have made all kinds of faces, for Gindler said, "Charlotte, why do you make such faces?"

I said, "I have such terrible pains in my legs."

"Oh," she said, "really? Stay standing. Maybe you find out how you create them."

I was terrified. But I kept at it, and by and by I realized what my legs were complaining about, and I found out what I was doing to create the pain.

When I was a child I was always held by the hand by the nurse. I wasn't allowed to do this, I wasn't allowed to do that. At last I was so intimidated that I hated every movement. The only thing which I wanted was reading and playing the piano. That was all. Nothing else. I was declared perfectly ungifted for anything which had to do with movement, and I believed it. But at last, in this work of sensing I realized I was only tightly held in, so held in by myself that I couldn't move; and I realized that all of what I thought was impossible for me was perfectly possible.

Interest in what is

CHARLOTTE: When we first wake up, we might feel how much we do to ourselves in not letting ourselves be free, simply hindering our own freedom. And the question would be, do we accept that as a beginning? Is it possible to feel something like that with the kind of interest a surgeon would have toward the condition of a person he operates on? Not with emotion. Not saying "how terrible!" but just in finding out what is. And then find out if we can become more permissive to what comes out of

55

'what is' at each moment—as we go along, gradually become freer for what happens. If we go on this discovery trip we actually may begin to experience how it is when we are giving to movement during a sensory experiment, and how it is when I'm resisting the helper who moves my leg or my head or whatever. How it is when I take over and do it myself. How it is when I just make myself flabby and let go. And how it is when I'm really awake and feel what happens. This is how you begin to work, how you begin to distinguish: Now I am too flabby; now I am resisting; now I'm taking over. It's interesting. Each bit of this is interesting. Neither right nor wrong. It's only different from moment to moment.

One or the other of you might say, "I cannot yet allow giving. I cannot yet allow somebody to carry my weight. I am still too watchful. I still have to hold." And you stay holding! It's an interesting discovery. After a little while when you get a little tired you may feel, "Maybe I could give a little bit more," . . . and you begin to give. It feels very good. Oh, it feels good! "Maybe I could allow it more often." And so we learn.

Who of you is either resisting, or helping, or pushing, or whatever? So what? Why not? You have to taste it. You must accept it. You must see that there is a world of resistance, there's a world of taking over and doing it yourself; there's a world of watching out, of constantly planning, and so on and on. By and by you will feel it's not necessary, and you will give it up. In fact, it gives itself up. But it will never give itself up when you don't recognize it. You have to recognize it and not punish yourself for it.

Staying with it

CHARLOTTE: You know, if you want to find out something you have to go after it. The student of Zen has to become quiet, and he has to persist in what he does no matter what. He is forced by his Zazen practice to sit in a certain posture for such and such time, and to concentrate on his breathing, and his breathing should be counted from one to ten. All this only in order to have the person stick with something over a large amount of time and not turn away from it, so that he actually gets himself into his own hands. That is, he becomes his own master, and at the same time he becomes his own servant.

Now when this question of posture and breathing is long enough persisted in—let me say for thirty years—then it can become so that everything falls into place by itself. The only person I know in San Francisco Zen Center who is really fully elastic is Suzuki Roshi himself, who is not any more holding his posture but is simply sitting. And you can see in his sitting how wonderfully moveable he is . . . and in his walking, and in everything he does, how fully he attends to everything he does.

Zen people count in periods of time where five days is not a long study period, and that thirty years is short. And so the dedication to Zen includes the agreement that at every moment one is available for years and years and years to what life offers. The sitting is an education toward full attending to everything which we happen to do—without thinking about it, just being in it. In this respect our work is very similar to Zen practice . . . the really being in what we do, not occupying our mind with other things but really being there for what happens to be.

So from morning to morning, in anything which might happen, you can be more fully with it, and you can leave your by-thoughts and your absent thoughts and your manipulations and all that does not belong, and come into a really deep contact with what you do—without putting any stress on it. One of my favorite sayings is from the medieval philosopher Paracelsus. He says, "Do what you have to do wholeheartedly. Don't take anything away from it, and don't add anything to it." Just imagine when we would live this way!

In order to be able not to make an effort—to come gradually into this state in which things can simply happen—one has to work. For instance, in reporting what has happened during an experiment. Yesterday [a student] was speaking about something, and suddenly her voice took an entire turn and became as though she was afraid to say what she was saying, as though she had lost the inner connection to it. I don't know whether the rest of you felt it. In such moments what you really want to communicate gets out of control and dissolves into a kind of confusion. When that happens, stick to it! Even if it is very puzzling, you know. Staying with it, not letting go of our intention, that's what we are working at here.

Or somebody says something and the hearer feels the tendency is not simply to speak out, but to become insistent. As though I want to convince somebody. As though the whole world is against me and I have to push it through! Yet nobody's against it. But even if somebody is against it, just to say it, just to have the inner connection with it. To simply let it out and that's it. Nothing added.

How is my breathing?

CHARLOTTE: What were we at last time? If you don't know, then you don't know what you work at.

STUDENT: We were at breathing in connection with movement: walking and then lying down and then walking again—and taking several steps. But for me, I really worked much more at this idea of becoming aware of breathing without having to think of breathing. Breathing becoming aware of me, kind of the other way around. And this last week I have had quite a few experiences where I wasn't watching, and breathing took over. Through that I also realized this tendency I have of pulling away. In walking, in sitting, I don't let my weight come through. And somehow I had this realization by way of breathing.

CHARLOTTE: How about the others? You know, this fishing in the dark must stop. You have to be very clear what you are working at.

STUDENT H: For me, it brought my breathing and myself closer together. It made me aware of something that's been happening the last few weeks. I find myself working faster than myself. I go beyond what I'm doing, so I'm not doing the very thing that I'm working on—whatever it is, from washing my hands to eating a bowl of cereal.

CHARLOTTE: You mean you are already ahead of yourself?

STUDENT H: Well, thinking of something else while I'm doing what I'm doing. But also doing it so quickly that I'm not doing it at all. Then I find my breath again, and I feel the water when I'm washing.

STUDENT J: I felt that in anything I had to do I had to be so changeable. . . to give it a chance. Even in breathing I have to wait. . . . instead of just going ahead and disregarding it in order to accomplish things. That way I wouldn't really feel what I did. As I would be doing something and kind of getting into it, I would interrupt myself and say,

"Oh, you're too slow," and lose touch with it, and then nothing would coordinate. I'm surprised how many times I had to change—to get back to breathing, to let it happen. And actually, though it seemed slower, if I allowed the time for it, it went really quicker.

CHARLOTTE: This would perhaps be the beginning of a new feeling in you. But imagine when you would have to do things at a great speed!

STUDENT J: I could still feel it. I was amazed that when I started noticing what I was doing I seemed to be going quite slowly, but when I would go back to my old ways I realized this new way is really faster.

CHARLOTTE: Is there anyone else? I'm not so much interested just now in what effect it had on you, but in what we were working on. Could you—instead of finding out what it did to you—first find out what we were working at? That's a most important thing. It takes often a long time until it becomes clear to us what we are working on. It's a very objective thing we are working on in the moment. Something you can see very clearly when you are able to get beyond yourself. In other words, not always asking, "What does it do to me?" but "What was I actually doing?"

STUDENT: I thought that part of the work we were doing was giving ourselves to the floor. Lying down and standing, and releasing energy to that. Not resisting or coming down without energy.

CHARLOTTE: Just a moment. I think it would be a very difficult thing for you to make anything out about this "giving myself to the floor." When you really lie down, that's enough. The moment you lie down you don't hold back anything. But in the moment you make out of it this "giving yourself to the floor" you come into difficulty. Because it is a very romantic and not a very matter-of-fact thing you describe. I meant lying down, really lying. Not pulling away and not collapsing.

STUDENT K: I remember one thing you said, Charlotte, about complete freedom in breathing, . . . going into sitting and everything else. You were saying, "Let breath come into your legs and arms."

CHARLOTTE: In what way did it strike you?

STUDENT K: I sort of cramp myself, and it made me feel more like coming out.

CHARLOTTE: You can look at the question from two different angles. One is, "Can I let my breathing be free?" The other would be, "Is my breathing with what is being said, or being done?" In other words, am I really—insidely—with what is happening right now? Yes? Then you are not any more "giving to your breathing" but your breathing gives to what is happening. It's there for it. In other words, instead of being egocentric you become social. You are there, and your inner functioning is there for what is just happening. It's a very healthy thing to get away from circling all the time around ourselves.

In the moment in which I'm available, one of the phenomena which I feel is that my breathing is also available. . . . So, when someone says he's ahead of himself, that means that—among other things—he is not really in contact with what he does, and, of course, his breathing is unconnected also. But I wouldn't think it would help too much when he begins then to rely on his breathing. He has to go to what he is doing. If he really comes to that, his breathing comes to it, too.

If you are too long only busy with your breathing, you make a god out of your breathing. And you will always stumble, wanting to get in contact with your breathing instead of getting in contact with what you are doing. If you relate to something, your breathing will relate to it.

STUDENT: I find it very difficult to be aware of my breathing, and let it happen. Once in a while breathing just starts. When I'm doing something, and I find myself breathing more, or less, then I become aware of breathing. But just to say, "Be aware of your breathing," I find very difficult.

CHARLOTTE: You have to get to both. What is the reason that we cannot allow an inner ease in letting something which is unconscious become conscious, without that we stagger in it? Without that we get anxious in it? But that instead we hear—and trust that our breathing hears too—in the moment when we really feel, "I am there for it." . . . When you have this kind of inner ease—without watching or pushing or saying "quick, quick, quick"—you have already more change. When you give up feeling obliged, this is already a fantastic thing. When you are working at becoming conscious of your breathing, why should you not have the inner peace to say, "I am there for it now. Whether I get conscious of it earlier or later is a secondary question. Whether it takes longer or not so long I don't care. I will wait it out." And you would be without any expectations and faithfully go about it. What comes, comes.

Make no fuss whatsoever about it and you will see what happens. If you are knowing in advance that it's difficult, so what? Then it's difficult.

I would like to give you for homework that you may say to yourself four or five times a day—no matter if you feel anything or not—just asking, "What can I feel of my breathing?" And then not rushing, but saying, "I'm not in a hurry at all, so I don't perform." You will find very often you perform, you right away begin to 'breathe'. That's not it. You might also feel you hold your breath. All right, you hold your breath, and at some time it will start again. You simply allow something which is vague to become a little more conscious. And not to influence it, but be grateful for anything you notice. And to give what is happening a few minutes' time for strengthening the connection between you and your breathing, . . . simply in staying it out, staying with something you want to find out about. You will feel when you do something to breathing, and you will give it up. You will feel when your breathing wants changes, and you will allow them. You will feel that here or there you need more breathing, and what happens then. So you can gradually become aware of the happenings. It strengthens your character very much. Makes you clearer in sensing. Makes you more honest.

The most important question would be, "Can I—without hurrying, without expecting anything—be fully in this? Without any romantic ideas, but like a scientist who is in an experiment?" Most important is the steadiness of this, and no romanticism at all. It needs objectivity to the last.

Now comes a second thing. Suppose you are reading. You want to be there for it. When you then begin to think of your breathing you are turning around something which will get you away from reading. You can't serve two masters. So, as you are reading, you can be there for it because what you read calls you, "Harriet!" "Peter!" "Ann!" You are not just reading, you are going with it. And all the time you are going with it your whole organism functions for it. Why should your breathing be left out? So it's no problem unless we interfere with it

Giving up doing

CHARLOTTE: When we do not function naturally, but instead make an effort to use our senses, we have the feeling we must do something. We do something in seeing, we do something in smelling, we do something in breathing. This is how we are educated, you know. When the mother says to the child, "Doesn't this taste good?" [*Charlotte makes lip-smacking sounds*] or "Listen to the airplane!" or "Look at this!" . . . Boom! Reaction sets in for the child. And the mother, with the best will in the world, begins to disorient and distort the sense-perception of the child. And it is aggravated when educators force a child to give answers immediately and to respond as "correctly" as possible. Much pressure is put upon the child to respond the way people want him to. He soon learns to feel he always should be doing something. But the important thing is that we have to give up doing. Now, how can one bring this under the skin of a person?

It is not so easy. People say, "I am working too hard. I am making too much effort. I have to let go." They call it 'relaxing'. But natural functioning cannot be recovered by just 'relaxing'. The organism has a marvelous way of reacting when one does too much: it creates restrictions and resistances which come from hard effort. Then the very fine, self-directing, and healing processes of the organism find everywhere these resistances, and this, by and by, makes these processes—let me say—a little numb. They gradually get what you could call resigned. They try and try. Always there is resistance. At last they give up.

Now when you would find a person who has built up such strong resistances through much effort, and he simply lets them go, then the rebuilding abilities of the organism—which had been numbed—do not right away start up again. The person stays numb and unalive and unvital, and it is often worse than before when the resistances were still there. This letting-go stuff is just mind-business, because if we would be present when we really have let go we would find out what a wet rag we are then, how we are depleted.

The change demands something quite different, . . . namely, as we are beginning to hinder less and less, we feel how, with the diminution of the resistances, the wells begin to flow again to fill up these gaps. And there, where the resistances hindered, gradually the life activities fill in, and so recovery happens. Can you go with me? Does this make sense to you?

When one has looked in order to see, has listened in order to hear, has smacked in order to taste, has made an effort in order to think, he doesn't know at all that he has constantly prevented the natural activities in his organism. So when I come to you with invitations to make more ease here or there, I mean not that you simply let go, but that this is a way, a path, which you can only take step by step. In this sense I would like you to feel, when you are in this work of transformation, that you are not using a technique but that when you follow anything you follow only the natural tendencies of the organism; the inner has to awake.

There is a kind of sensitivity, a boundless awakeness, and when you are not using these calculated efforts any more, and not constantly going around with your thoughts, you become much more awake and much more really to the point, because then you can experience. When your mind is full with all kinds of effort and thought, it's like when you go to a lavatory and there is a sign which says, "Occupied." You can't enter because it's occupied with something else. So when this invitation comes to you to permit the thoughts gradually to come to more rest, then it is that the positive forces can come in and restore you while your efforts decrease. Then your head clears like the sky, and at the end of it you are crystal clear and feel fully awake and wonderfully free, and everything in you functions.

This would be the understanding when you enter the study of sensing, that you only gradually lose the numbness, . . . losing that which prevents your organs from functioning. What we have to offer you is nothing but that you begin to give up what is hindering you, and you become a little more normal. That you strain less to see, for example. And if you cease to make this effort, then you will no longer feel as if you see with your eyes, but that everything simply comes in and influences you.

What is most to be understood is that when I am sensing, my head is entirely free of any intention to sense. I am simply functioning. I think we are too much supervising, too much directing. Who understands that? Who was able to do a little less of that today? How does it feel to you when you are not supervising any more?

STUDENT K: Very surprising. Things happen you don't expect. It's an entirely different way to me of feeling

CHARLOTTE: What is the difference? I mean we have to take our time with this now. Because you are just going over a new threshold. Each one of you. This is something which doesn't happen in the unconscious. It comes to consciousness, and only then does it become significant for us, because we begin to understand something of the organism's functioning, when we experience it differently. What is the difference? What was the difference for you when you were in it?

STUDENT K: One thing which I felt strongly was how much . . . sounder to trust this than to always be saying, "Do this, feel that, put your head this way." The directing part. This feels so much sounder. It is subtle, and the other—this directing that I have done so much of—is so stiff and rigid.

CHARLOTTE: We speak so much of growth. How can we grow when there is a part in us which directs? How can we speak of growth when we always need a caretaker, so to say? It's as though we feel impotence everywhere and somewhere is potency, and we try to irrigate from the potency into the impotent part. Instead of realizing that everywhere is potency. Everywhere is this possibility.

STUDENT L: Someone spoke of trust, and . . . .

CHARLOTTE: No, wait a minute. . . . What occurred to you when you were in the experiment?

STUDENT L: I felt that I was sort of directing, expecting certain things that I have experienced before, watching. I don't know at what point it left off, but then I became much more moveable and flexible than before. And then it occurred to me: why can't I trust this?

CHARLOTTE: You felt it.

STUDENT L: Yes. Why do I do this to myself? Because I know I am doing it. I am imposing a rigidity that's not necessary.

CHARLOTTE: Can you feel with her, that something like this can happen in a person?

STUDENT M: Yes, I experienced the flexibility between the different members of my organism—flexibility between the different areas of bone.

CHARLOTTE: Now, wait a minute. Say what occurred to you. Just say what you felt while you were in the experiment. I saw a lot, so don't say anything which you didn't feel. Say exactly what you felt.

STUDENT M: I felt myself turning from one lump into something with many individual bones.

CHARLOTTE: Who felt bones?

STUDENT M: I didn't feel them, Charlotte, but I became aware of them. I felt able to flex. They weren't all knotted together, like made of one solid thing; they were divided into different areas. And I became a little bit aware of the flexibility, just aware of the flexibility of the human being. Very interesting, Charlotte. A few classes ago—

CHARLOTTE: No, no! Stay here.

STUDENT M: It's very interesting because I experience a kind of transparency where everything became so delicate and light that—

CHARLOTTE: Don't mix it here. As much as you might feel it delightful, forget it. You won't forget it, but I say, forget it. At one point you felt more transparency. That's possible, very possible, but get those other things out of there. I still think we are all dwelling too much on things from formerly, expecting this or that to happen. When you are in a real experience you don't sail off and think that what you imagine is more important than what you feel. Feel what happens, and also say what happens. And leave out all the things you think. Compare your sensation with your words and if it isn't fitting exactly, then seek for another word until it covers what you felt.

Because I am a good friend of yours, I have to stop you short, because I feel that very much of what you say is already beyond the actual experience. Recalling similar experiences or wondering what this experience might mean only keeps you from having the experience. It's a smearing between experience and fantasy. Someday maybe we could come to really say, "My experience is enough—so much so that I am nearly overcome by it!" It is so rich when one really is there for it. One doesn't talk about this and that in one's head, but one feels, ... and it will be a very unusual language which you begin to speak.

Did you feel how others were looking for words? They said it didn't come very easily because they were feeling back in their experience, and it said itself in a way in which they usually don't speak. That's how it becomes creative. It never should sound cute. It will sound marvelous as soon as somebody is close to an experience.

When you demand that, you get so clear, you get so sharp. You get so close to things that all this fogginess inside you leaves. Even when you say, "I felt nothing," it's much better than when you build up a beautiful castle and are just a little bit off what is happening. You keep your teeth in it. You don't let it go until you have what was really so. You understand? You keep your teeth in the bone like a dog. And so you keep with your experience, maybe saying "No, this was not quite how it was," and giving it time in yourself to feel that it can be recovered and comes really out as what you felt and nothing else. And then when somebody should prosecute you, you would say, "Here I am. Here I stand. I cannot say it differently." Do you see? This is a quite different kind of life. It's difficult, but it's possible.

I had a student who was also a student of the fashion designer, Dior, in Paris. Dior would have the model stand before him with the amount of material, and he would take the material and drape it on her, and then he would take a pin and pin it there. And he would go back to see it, like a painter very often does when he has made a stroke. He would say, "No, it has to go more this way," and he would take the pin out, take the material a little bit more this way. And he would use a half an hour so that he would be satisfied with it—that his sense of what he really wanted to bring out was fulfilled.

Now you don't have to bring out anything. You are already created, you know, and you are beautifully created. Only, you can live so that the creation which you are is unrecognizable, and one doesn't know who you are, . . . and you don't know who you are because you are so full of habits and what other people have told you. So what we have to do now is to bring you into a state of curiosity and deep interest for what gradually may emerge out of this sum of many conditionings, . . . so that you could feel, "That's me, unmistakably. Now I speak. I'm not repeating anything which somebody else says. This is what I really have to say; this is what I really have to do; this is how I connect with another person; this is how I approach my task, no matter how difficult it is. Now I can feel it. Now I can gradually come more to the bottom of it."

We have created in ourselves many barriers . . . as a kind of self-defense. For instance, people don't listen any more; there's too much talk. People get lukewarm about things; there's too much to get alerted for. People close up against experiences and stay on the surface; they can't stand this assault of all kinds of things which come toward them. People are flabby and listless; they have given up, often through experiences which go far back into their childhood. They have given up being interested, so often they were forbidden to be interested. And things like that.

Today is not then: today is today

CHARLOTTE: So our behavior today is very often the result of conditioning we have received in early times, and we have never understood that today we could go about living differently. In other words today is not then, long ago, but today is today. And today is not only today; this hour is this hour and this minute is this minute and this second is this second and this split-of-a-second is this split-of-a-second.

In any moment in which we are living we can be there for what is going on and have our energy mobilized for what we are doing. That would be a healthy living. In the moment when we are not any more clinging to the past, but are letting ourselves be free for what is happening now, we function. There is no room any more for holding back or being lukewarm or all these different manifestations of a protection against something which may not at all exist now. And in case we actually need to protect ourselves now we can do it openly. We can protect ourselves in freedom instead of carrying all this constriction which pretends to protect us.

Very often conditions are so built into us that they are like our second nature—so strong that they have become unconscious, and we don't feel them any more. At first when we do something to ease ourselves and come more into the neighborhood of our real nature we may not feel the changes yet. There may still be resistance deep down in the tissues to what we want to allow, and we may not feel that it resists. But by and by thawing sets in and rigidity gradually gives up. Then we begin to feel what we are doing. We become sensitive.

Honoring everything with our inner attention

CHARLOTTE: When once you see—really see—somebody who has sensitivity, you can never miss it. I remember a Hindu dancer doing a temple dance. He was standing. He drank out of a cup. And then he sat down. That was all! I will never forget what happened to me while he was sitting down. He didn't do anything else . . . nothing . . . and I suddenly realized what sitting means. Nothing else but this simple movement of coming to sitting. One felt that this man was absolutely there for it. There was a real electric quality in it, . . . at the same time the greatest peace and the most beautiful movement you could imagine. The whole big auditorium of people were absolutely breathlessly following this one motion. He came to sitting and sat. There was a dead silence. Then a kind of tumult started. Everybody was delirious with excitement, and rushed forward, wanting to get near this dancer.

Such things happen. What we allow of sensitivity is closely connected with love, and innocence. A person who is self-conscious cannot allow. It must come out of the direct contact of our real inner connection, without breaks.

I don't know whether any of you is so far as to feel what actually is happening in these classes. I give away the secret: it is to allow everything one does, really. We have chosen the most simple things which we do all the time, to feel out to which degree we honor everything with our inner attention.

In China there's a saying which calls lying, sitting, standing, and walking the four dignities of man. When we are babies we do them all fully. You know, when you see a child sitting, it's perfect. It is sitting. When you see an adult sitting usually it's no sitting. He has thrown that away. It doesn't concern him.

We have this marvelous ability to sense, this wonderful equipment of sensing. And we don't have to think about it; we have it all in us. Every person has gone through the stages of sitting, of standing. The discovery by a baby of standing is one of the most wonderful things to watch. How often he falls, how often he cannot come completely up. And in each time the same delight . . . and struggle. He is trying to get up until at last, when he is standing, he beams with delight. This satisfaction of arriving at something which is really 'it' is inborn in us. We feel it immediately when we come into the neighborhood of 'it'. That's 'it'!

Now, what has impressed me so exceedingly with my teacher, Elsa Gindler, was that whatever she did she did fully. And whatever was being done was subject enough for her feeling it out and fulfilling it. Not thinking about it but actually permitting it to happen. For instance, Elsa Gindler would sit and turn a page in a book which was lying before her—without that she would pay any attention to it consciously, and the way she turned the page was one hundred percent. It was so beautiful to see. It was not what we usually call graceful. It was just 'it'. She was fully in the moment, and when she let the page come to lying there you had the feeling that she took care of it—without thinking about it—in the same way in which she would take care of the most precious thing she had.

We cannot judge things, dividing them into two kinds: one which doesn't concern me, doesn't interest me, that goes without my paying attention to it. The others—the so-called higher things or deeper things—which I think are interesting, and devote myself to. When this judging gradually stops, and instead we would give each thing we do the same honor, then it would be quite different.

In Zen they say, "When I drink, I drink; when I'm angry, I'm angry; when I sit, I sit; when I sleep, I sleep." You know? Undivided. Just it. And in this way I would like you to understand what we are doing here. In the moment in which the orchestra of the human being—our many dimensionality—would give itself in a united way to action, then we would function. Who realizes that sensing has a right of its own? You can simply follow it.

I like always to speak about how 'it' wants to be. In other words, the message comes from inside without that you have any idea in your head about how it should be. For instance, when you are interested in a person, you don't have to think about it—you feel it, you know? You don't have to think about whether the water is cold or warm; you feel it. You don't have to think about whether a situation is difficult or not, you feel it. So, is it possible to simply react immediately, spontaneously, to what's happening? So that the whole living person is automatically reacting to what's happening? Then it's easy. Then it makes fun. Then you begin to trust your own sensations, and can simply follow your perceptions.

Allow what is happening to move you

CHARLOTTE: Every day brings very different moments, and in every moment there is a possibility of responding or not responding. And we can be there and discover that. Our energy can become very powerful at times when we need to have powerful energy, and can become very easy when at times we need to have less. So the energy flow and the possibility of perseverance and strength is constantly changing in us according to what we are meeting in the moment.

There's a difference when you swim through a lake which is quiet and when you swim against a very strong current. That is terribly hard to do, you know, but one gets a lot of energy from it. This is the energy which I instinctively like, and which we all like so much in children. To go against something which is powerful, . . . going against it, you know, for fun. You don't make work of it. You don't say, "Now I'm breathing very deep, now I'm sitting really straight." It comes by itself. You just climb a mountain and see how it is when you are going higher and higher. And in doing so you are being furnished with what you need. You don't have to exercise yourself, make effort.

We have this kind of inner variability, this adaptability, these many phases of energy which are provided by nature. This richness, in other words. And we have it also in emotional ways. To be able to be from hearty laughing to deep crying. All the different phases of human responses

But a father often says, "A strong girl shouldn't so easily cry." Or, "You are a boy! Don't become a sissy!" So we hold back. Erich Fromm, with whom I worked a great deal when he was in New York, once called me and said, "Charlotte, I have a woman here. I want to work with her, but I can't because she is absolutely immovable. You work with her." So this woman came to me. A beauty! An Englishwoman, very good family, you know, very beautiful person. But. . . she never changed the expression of her face. And I said to her, "How about that?" She said, "We were beaten as children when we changed the expression of our face. We were not permitted to laugh or cry, so we had always to keep a straight face." How many people are educated like this? Often, in having a 'good education' one learns to be a particular way, and then that's the way you are for life.

This workshop will, I hope, permit you to see how it is when you experience what you do and what you say. . . . That you actually allow to go under your skin what others say, so you can experience it. That you don't just hear it and have some thoughts about it and let it go, but that you actually allow whatever is happening to move you. Instead of hearing it intellectually, 'understanding' it as we say, and, with that, it's finished. I would say that there is no understanding without the experience which has preceded it. We cannot really understand when we don't experience what we go through, . . . what we hear, what we see, and so on. When the experience is not allowed, we do not understand. We only think we understand, but we do not understand

Who felt, for instance, that the slapping we did for each other in our last experiment went deeper than just to the skin and the first tissue layer behind the skin? You know, I often say that the back is the room between the skin of the back and the floor . . . when one lies on one's stomach. So it's going through if you allow it, if you are awake for it. And it is not confined to the surface. Who felt this already when you were being slapped, that it goes further than just to the skin and the layer right behind the skin? . . . Yes?

Student: I did, but I felt sad. I sit here and I keep feeling sadder. And I don't know why. But this afternoon we put our hands on our heads where we thought our thinking was done, and then afterward we put our hands over our eyes, and you said, "Those who are putting their fingertips over their eyes can put the palms of their hands over their eyes and see if they fit." And when I did, tears came. But I don't know why.

Charlotte: Are you glad that it came? It may be just a reaction, a first reaction of the work, you know, that you feel more deeply what's happening. And that overawes you. Very possible. So it might not be that it is sadness, but it might be that it's a reaction to what is happening there, perhaps for the first time in your life since you can remember . . . that you begin to react.

Many people weep their hearts out. They have to weep and weep because so much of repressed weeping is in us, and so much is held back in us which might want to come to life and express itself. So this is very important that you do not hold back then, like some people when they have to yawn. They do all kinds of things to hide the yawning. Who did that today? And didn't let the yawn come fully through so that it can express itself? This is the freedom which allows us more natural expression and to experience deeper what we are feeling.

I remember when I was studying with Elsa Gindler we worked on breathing. And for the first time I became conscious of the fact that it came by itself, and I didn't have to do anything about it. It was an enormous, overwhelming shock for me, and an overwhelming feeling of happiness that it came by itself and functioned by itself. And I didn't have to do anything for it. That's probably the first time that I got a glimpse of what it is to function.

And what a fantastic experience it can be when one doesn't always have the feeling one has to do something to function. That was the great message which Elsa Gindler gave us. She said, "You have it all. You have it all, but you have to permit it and not hinder it. When you give up hindering it you will be fine."

One of my students once made a very interesting statement. She said, "In some way I have to have myself at least a little bit in control, because if I would let that go, what would happen?" And she meant it, you know. If she would let this control go, what would happen? She had not yet experienced—and I don't think that many of us do—that, in the moment in which one actually is there for something, that something sets the stage.

Every task sets the stage. You don't have to set it. In the moment in which you are open for it you see all that belongs to it, and your potentials are there with what you need, That's the great wonder of the organism. The question is whether you allow it.

Let it carry you

STUDENT: For the last couple of days . . . I've been aware of pain in my legs, just a sort of dull awareness of it. Then I could feel a letting-go in my hips and thighs. It was difficult to really let the weight go down. But as I could let go, my legs started really feeling good.

CHARLOTTE: So, she has been holding herself in the hips and thighs. Who has discovered something similar, could give it up to a certain degree? [*A few students raise their hands.*] You know, these unnecessary holdings come from lack of balance. We usually stand either too much forward or backward, and our muscles must grip, otherwise are would fall. In other words, we don't give our weight enough downward, and unconsciously we use our muscles to hold us up from falling. So what she felt was the effort of her muscles which held her up from falling. But then she found more the place where she could simply balance, and she didn't need this muscle effort any more. So it felt good.

I remember one incident when I studied with Gindler: this same question was acute, and she realized some of us still did lip service to this matter of giving to the support of the floor or the earth, when actually we held ourselves fervently up. We were in Switzerland, on a beautiful lawn with trees, and Gindler wanted us to go up on a big tree branch and stand there. And I remember that it took me about five minutes until I dared. I was on my hands and knees. I was trembling all through, and everything was just tense in me, and I didn't dare to stand up. Then at last—after I took a little more courage—I came up, but I was still very frightened. Gindler stood next to me and said, "Now this is a wonderful occasion to find out: do you really permit what is under you—this branch—to carry you? Or do you hold yourself on it?" I felt I was holding like hell. And I still was trembling all over . . . it was just violent! And then she said, "Now, stay. Just give yourself a little time to feel whether you couldn't more and more come to standing on it. Let it carry you. You don't need to hold yourself on it." And sure enough, by and by my excitement went away and my muscles began to give up the unnecessary tension, and at last I was standing on this thing perfectly freely. I had a wonderful feeling of balance. And it was such a huge difference between this first not even daring—clinging to this piece of wood high up in the air and not daring at all—and then gradually coming to it.

STUDENT: My legs were tight and wouldn't give up holding on. I can bend my knees and let go of where I hold in my thighs, . . . but then I'm not in balance. I feel like there's got to be more tone, some tension in those muscles.

CHARLOTTE: You know sailboats, don't you? Where there's no wind, the sail gets slack. The breeze or the wind is constantly doing something to the sails. And our muscles in front and back and on the sides, inside and outside, could be constantly moved by the inner breeze. By breathing, in other words. And would neither get tight nor get slack but would be all the time massaged through by breathing. Getting smaller and larger and smaller and larger through breathing.

Being re-formed by breathing

CHARLOTTE: In the last session we touched the front and the back of the shoulder area of a partner. And you probably noticed that there's something living inside. There is something going on in us which could constantly form us: the excursions of breathing.

While breathing is happening—and it's happening all the time— the inner tissues are being formed by what comes in and what goes out. And the more delicate our tissues are to this forming capacity of our breathing—to this refreshing, renewing capacity of our breathing—the more will we come into a posture which is sensitive and reactive and open for what is constantly being a creative power in us.

When your breathing is very hindered, then you will easily collapse and fall together because you are not reacting to this possibility of allowing the air to form you. When your breathing is more creative— when you are not closing yourself against it—then there is a possibility of being constantly re-formed by breathing.

When we occupy ourselves further with this source of life, breathing, we find out to which degree we are, in our structure, shaped for it. The lungs are very nicely embedded inside our upper chest, reach quite down and are distributed like two sponges through the front and back and sides of our rib cage. In the middle is the chest bone, a bone which by nature could be somewhat elastic. And from both sides of the chest bone originate cartilage which is elastic, . . . which is then followed by the ribs, which are also elastic by nature. And between the different ribs are muscles which are connecting one rib with the other and which are permissive to the in-and-out-going air.

So that's the structure. The lungs distribute to the sides in our chest, also the lower chest, and the lung tips lie up in the neighborhood of the powerful muscles which go from the neck over to the arm, where so many people have trouble: the shoulder musculature. And this shoulder muscle, which is very powerful, lies very well in the valley of bones which hold them very friendly. They come down and continue on both sides— a little bit toward the back—to the arm. You can easily feel them with your fingers. With most of us they are as hard as iron, but they don't have to be.

And the lung tips, the very last ends of our lungs—which are exceedingly delicate, exceedingly fine friends—they are going into the neighborhood of this powerful muscle, and of course you can imagine how hard a time they have when the muscle holds tight against them. They cannot allow the air and the reactions to the movement of breathing really, because there is a stiff muscle on top of them which is so resistant. It is very important for us to feel in our arms and through our shoulder-blade area that this powerful muscle which comes down and spreads out is not jammed by the way we are holding our shoulders high or are pushing our head down. And we are often very constricted in our upper arms. So this possibility of the refined activities of the lung tips depends on the permissiveness of our upper extremities to allow elasticity so the air can flow where it wants to flow. So the first thing which is very important in breathing is that one permits musculature to give rather then to be held constricted.

STUDENT: When we lay down and covered our eyes, at one point I realized that I hadn't breathed for a long time, my breath really just stopped. And I waited for that, and then that new breath was like a new breath of life.

CHARLOTTE: That's what I would like you all to realize. When your breathing doesn't continue that you let it not continue, that you give it rest, so to say. You allow it to be not continuing until something happens by itself. In other words, you don't get nervous and then take a breath, but you let it have its own way of stopping and of starting out again by itself. It's not that you start it.

For instance, when breathing stops for a while after exhalation, then there is a wonderful chance that everything in the organism finds its place. I don't know whether you realize that when exhalation is really allowed more fully that it has a great releasing, a real resting quality in it. When exhalation comes, and goes on and on and on, let it. Let it be. And then, by itself, the wings, so to say, lift, and a new breath begins to start. That's one of the most delicious feelings one can have. I can't advertise enough that you try this out.

You know, there are in India people who test their strength in trying out how long they can stop their breath, how long they can exhale. In the West we are always nervous. . . . We often interrupt our breathing right in the middle of exhalation in order to get a new breath through. Forget it. Allow the rhythm of breathing to be entirely as it wants to be. And when it's shallow, let it be shallow. Don't criticize it.

If in the organism here and there something begins to become hungry for air or hungry for cleaning, it will show up and breathing will come to help and allow then what is needed. But for that we have to become more awake, insidely.

When you really become sensitive, then you lose your constrictions. Because tissue which is still constricted is not yet quite sensitive. I cannot give you a kiss when my lips are at the same time tight, or it is a tight kiss. This is clear? If I want to give you a kiss my lips must be free for it. That means that if I want to feel you in kissing I must be free in my lips. I can't embrace anybody fully and at the same time hold myself tight. I cannot clean the dishes and be tight in my arms and in my neck or shoulders. If I do so I will suffer. But if I clean the dishes and am free for it, it feels like a dance. It's beautiful. Every motion comes free out of us and we can really enjoy what we do.

Part IV: Sensing Is Coming in Contact with What We Do

CHARLOTTE: Sensing is getting more in touch with oneself, with others, and with the world. We are offering to you a work which, in its very character, somehow embraces our possibility of getting in touch with whatever we do or whomever we meet—and going as deeply as possible into this coming-in-contact-with-what-we-do.

Everything is being-in-touch or coming-in-touch, not only in massage or in catching a ball, but also in speaking, or in solving a difficult problem, or in having a great deal of fun. It's all a question of to which degree I am burning for it, so to say, am there for it, and what consequences it has in me. In the way you connect—it doesn't make any difference in what activity—anything you do embraces the whole universe. If the connection is poor, it is poor. You will feel it and it will bring you to become a little more fully participating, because in the moment you feel it's not quite satisfying to you, then you are on the way to something which is more contact. Anything you would feel is not quite 'it' leads you more to 'it'. This is one of the most wonderful things which we can be grateful for.

It is not in the way that we do an exercise, that we do it well or not well, but that we instead become conscious of our approach to the world. I was no longer in Germany at the end of World War II when the bombing was tearing up the whole city of Berlin, and many of the inhabitants, too. But during this time people in this work tested it: they discovered how they reacted to this very dangerous situation with all its enormous tasks. I have letters from some of these people who said that they were functioning better and could be more fully there for the things which they did and which they encountered.

So we have here, now, this quiet studio and this beautiful environment. In a way it is beautiful that we have it, but in another way it may mislead us into thinking that we can only function when everything is quiet and beautiful around us, when that is really not so. Every moment offers itself in its own way, and the question is how I answer it.

When I was a young girl I made a trip on a train and I met an entire stranger. And that man had the nerve to say to me, "I have loved most those women whose names I don't remember, with whom I have been together only once." I thought it was an interesting statement. He got out at the next station and I wondered who he met that evening.

So, in the flash of a moment you can make a friend—or you can also be entirely on the surface. When we are a little bit more open we have a very much more interesting life. To allow a direct connection, no matter whether it is with our beloved or it is with a woman in the market, or it's with the vegetables which we buy, or it's with I don't know what— the ball which we catch and throw—we can always have just a surface connection, or we can instead live deeply in this moment for what we happen to meet.

Now, if you are not present and don't know it, nobody can help you. But if you feel it, then the next move would be to allow that which would make more contact possible, with the possibility of a greater effect through the whole of you. But we very often are too lazy to allow that, or we are too vain to allow that. Or Mother has said, "What you do in the first moment must always be right," so you insist that this is right no matter what you feel.

Learning to follow our sensing

CHARLOTTE: Now, if all this dirt from the past drops away from you and you meet what you feel now, perfectly new, you are grateful for noticing, "Aha! I close myself here." And if, with pure heart, so to say, without reproaching yourself in any way, you allow a little more opening, you might feel then "Yes, but it's not yet open enough," and you would allow still a little bit more opening. You might still feel, then, "It's not yet open enough," and you would again allow another change. Then you might feel, "My! It's too open now!" and you would go back a little bit. And that's the way we learn to follow our sensing.

You have to have tenderness not to disturb this. You don't stare and say, "What's this?" There is only a very sensitive feeling-out. And when you feel it out like this you discover that what you sense is never just a psychological thing or just a physical thing, because the psychological and the physical can't be separated. You feel it together. You sense it. Sensing always has both in it.

When what we are doing is important for us, why do we build up so many unnecessary resistances? When once we see that we really want something, then we get going. We all have too much the feeling that we can choose. We do choose, but the best choices are made when we are simply in a thing, doing what we are doing with our whole selves. Trying to choose only puts us in friction with ourselves. We spend so much time in our lives wanting something and going against it at the same time, but when once we realize perfectly clearly, "I want this!" then much of that friction falls away. It's true we can't will it to happen, but when you feel the inner yearning, give to it.

You will realize that when you are sensitive you go only as far as you can. No one will ever get so much that it can't be digested. When you are overflowing with emotion, that is too much; you will get all mixed up with it. But when you are really sensitive you get only what you can digest. The very nature of sensitivity is reactivity, and we will not take too much. When you are sensitive you don't overeat. When you are sensitive you don't become an alcoholic. You can't, because your inner measure warns you.

When you are sensing and you would need a little more time, take that time. Don't stop so short that you destroy the possibility of sensing or make too important what is cut off. This is an art which we have to learn, . . . to be so permissive in sensing the situation that we don't aggravate it or bring some other element into it. Our sensing must be like the most delicately sensitive friend, who always knows when to be absent and always knows when to be present, with a presence which is never obtrusive. Our sensing can aggravate the situation if it turns to critical observation. Instead, there must be the finest possible touch in it so that the organism doesn't feel criticized.

It's really very easy, getting tuned in, getting more available for what you are doing. Let's say [a student] is standing and cooking. She feels suddenly that she holds tightly in her legs. When she feels it, she can sense what this holding has to say. When she has sensed it she can allow what wants to change in her so the holding can disappear and she can be there for the cooking. It sounds very simple, and it is very simple! As a matter of fact, when Elsa Gindler came out with this we all just hit our heads against the wall and said, "Why did we have to work so long!"

When one has always held oneself back from contact it feels like an adventure not to hold back any more. And when one gets into contact with something, is busy with something, this is a very strong boat which carries you. When one really has contact with what he is busy with, he is taken care of. One is never alone, never alone. One is always in contact with what one happens to be with. With silence, for instance, or whatever it is.

Getting away from choosiness

STUDENT N: All the time you've been talking I was thinking that, in times of crisis, it seems so easy to have the inside and the outside working right close together. Is that because we forget ourselves?

CHARLOTTE: Yes. We are more heightened.

STUDENT N: And then there's no choice. We just act.

CHARLOTTE: Then there's no question. I do believe that when things really become urgent—suppose this house is burning—it hits through to your very core. When anything hits us through to the very core, there is no person any more.

STUDENT N: But one can't live by crisis alone.

CHARLOTTE: I would say that, for me, every moment is acute. That means that when I'm busy with something I let it go to my heart. I think this happens for all of us when we get away from choosiness. For in choosing we don't let things become so close that we live in them.

Actually, something is always happening. People who don't love the moment are always trying to achieve something, but, when one is on the way, every moment of the way is 'it'. There is no achievement necessary because one goes forward anyhow. Every moment fills up or deepens a relationship, and then one doesn't need any more this constant trying to come to something. Choosing to do this, trying to do that. None of that is necessary. When I'm working with you the phenomena interest me very much, but when I get ambitious for you, everything goes wrong.

I wish you would once in awhile look into the eyes of a healthy baby, and would see with what earnestness, interest, great power of concentration—a basic saying yes—such a child has. The child doesn't yet want anything special; it is equally interested in everything that comes. When the child takes something and looks at it from all sides, or when somebody goes through the room and the child's whole attention follows, that's how we started. And it is also what we can come to— when this natural inner drive for full relating is unearthed and set free. We wouldn't be all the time so full of expectations and wishes, but we would be seeing more clearly that any world in which we live can be as astonishing as the world of the baby. And then all things are precious.

During lunchtime the other day, there were two little children sitting opposite me, eating. It was unbelievable to see how they were eating— fully there for their eating. And the eyes were just like little lakes, you know. Open. Perfectly free. And they didn't fill themselves. They ate one bite after the other, and it was all bliss. Then, when I came away from lunch, I sat by the path—right next to it—and a young mother with a little toddler came along. The mother was walking before, in front of the child. There were these big trees, and the green meadow, and the shadows thrown on the road. And the child was constantly stopping to look from one thing to the other, to the other, to the other, and so on. Took everything in with such an intensity! Her little hands were spread, you know. She was all-seeing. Sometimes she'd walk a few steps; then she'd turn around and look over to me. Then she'd turn again around, look over to the trees. And it was difficult for her to follow her mother.

There was another thing: the road—rather stony. And she was walking over this road, and sometimes, when a stone was in the way, she would stand a little bit back and then go over the stone. She didn't evade it. She went over it and came down again. And you could see in her little steps that she was conscious of what she was walking on. She hadn't learned it; it came all by nature. I was fascinated; I learned from her. There seems to be something basic in us which can teach us much— much more than one could learn by being told—about what we could practice, and what we could say about it. And I think we should trust that basic something.

Being open to self and other—the inner and the outer

CHARLOTTE: You can only get clear through practice. Nobody can tell you anything about that. You practice, and then you begin to feel a little more, and by and by you can speak about it. But to speak always about ourselves, and to think always about ourselves, we waste an enormous amount of time. I am sorry to say it, but you know, we are too touchy about ourselves. When you have a hardship, let the hardship speak to you, and allow the changes so that there's less hardship. Otherwise we are constantly circling around ourselves. What is needed is that we give ourselves to a task.

Today you have been hearing all the reactions to yesterday's experiments. Now, first of all, do you talk your experience, or do you come out with it? What is 'talk' and what is 'speaking out'? Second, did you have the feeling today that what was said here was talked to death, or to life? We can have an attitude so that our ears just let it come a little bit into our brain, and that's the end of it. On the other hand, I'm sure that those who did attend yesterday were very much moved by what was said. You came to life, you experienced with each one who spoke, you experienced within yourself what was happening to the one who was speaking. And that's the most precious thing in the world.

We can think the work has only to do with what is going on in us, inside us. And we can become carried away by this inner excitement, and we can stay entirely with ourselves. "Am I sitting right? Is my head free? Is my neck elastic?" And so on. You can see the participation is not true. It's an egocentric existence. Be careful about that. When another speaks, live with the other. Creep under the skin of the other, if possible. This would be the way to become alive and open.

So, every flutter of a change in the other person would become fascinating to you, and you would feel it in yourself, what's happening in the other. Otherwise, we are only caring for our own house, and we are in danger of becoming narcissistic. Who feels this danger? Be very careful about that.

I find this fascinating, that I sit here and when I see you I feel me. You can feel me, too, and you can feel everybody here. A question is, do you, when you speak, include everybody here? Do you take notice of this human situation, that there are thirty people who want to hear what you say, including Charlotte, who has a hearing problem? The question is: how do we meet problems? I had a student who couldn't continue to work with me. She wrote me later, saying she had divorced her husband, "I couldn't live with him because he didn't go with the flow of life." The flow of life, she said, was what she wanted!

Life does not flow in any particular way, you know, but in the moment I can accept that it doesn't flow always the way I want I can allow gradually a little more and a little more the possibility to meet it as it is. Then, perhaps through this allowing, conditions change. Because I have a reaction, too, I am not a nothing. How I feel about my environment will be felt by it, too. Everybody of us, in hearing what the other person has to say, goes away enriched by what everybody else has experienced— if it is allowed in. That doesn't mean you lose yourself. It means you use all of your faculties, all of yourself. We are much richer in this possibility of meeting the world than we think we are.

When I was in Japan, I met a girl who had spent several years in an ashram in the United States, and two years in Japan. She was very beautiful, but she sat all the time with her eyes closed. She said she was listening to her inner music. We were on a train, travelling through a most interesting landscape, but she saw nothing of it. I asked her how she felt about the many sad things that were happening in the world today, and if she did anything about them. She said, "Before I can do anything for anyone else, I must first find out more about myself." Imagine! For nine years she had been trying to find out about herself, going through the world with her eyes closed!

To be sensitive is not just to be sensitive to what is inside you, but to what is outside of you, too. If we are sensitive, we cannot be sensitive just to how our spine moves. We are also sensitive to what is happening outside us, and then we do what is in us to do. We can only offer what we have. Whether anyone accepts it is another matter. We have to take a chance with that.

STUDENT: I think housework is something that I feel does not take all of me, does not use all of what I have. I must do the housework, but I feel sometimes that what really interests me, or what makes me feel alive, is something else.

CHARLOTTE: Now, let me recall a discussion which Elsa Gindler had with a good friend of mine, also a teacher of this work. She had two sons and a husband—three men. She had constantly to mend stockings, mend underwear, besides all the other housework. She mentioned that she turned on the radio when she was mending and listened to good music. And then the mending became doubly good. Elsa Gindler stopped her and said, "What?" For two hours Elsa Gindler tried to get my friend to understand that there was something lacking, that she actually did not give herself to the mending, that she did not give the mending a chance to become a way of practice—"a way of unfolding," Gindler called it.

You see, when we are not interested, nothing can happen. When we have resistances, then what we call 'happening' can't happen. Very often we don't discover our resistances consciously, and that's why sensing is so important. Because, in the moment you begin to feel more clearly what condition you are in, you can feel—in the condition—what brings it about. For instance, when you really feel yourself in the condition which you described, you can sense what brings it about. There must be a remnant of something in you which prevents you from being all there for the housework, and this points at something which is either animosity in this moment, or something which has happened in the past and is still lingering in you—or possibly a worry about the future. When you feel yourself in this situation, you can sense what it is saying to you.

You know, you cannot apply the work. When you apply the work, you will always go wrong. In the moment in which you peel a potato, it has only to do with the potato and you. What the work can do is make you so desirous of contact, make you so able to make contact, make you so loving, so sensitive, that a different kind of connection can come about between you and the potato you peel. Nobody can teach you that. What the work can do is to make you so aware of the superficiality of your usual contact that you cannot stand it any more, and your inner demands a different quality of contact. But that is all spontaneous. In the last effect, the work makes you hungry for real contact.

Relating to people

CHARLOTTE: Two years ago in Tassajara, there was a man who was about fifty-six years old, a very successful professional who worked with people. We were playing with balls. We each had a ball in our hands, really permitting the presence of the ball to influence us. And then we gave our ball to someone else. The man gave his ball to somebody, and when he was empty-handed he went on, and by and by somebody else gave him their ball. At one moment the man broke down in tears and couldn't hold back his weeping. He went into a corner and wept and wept. I didn't say anything.

And then just last week we received a letter from him saying, "When I gave the ball away and I received a ball, I realized that I had never given or received anything until then." . . . So, you know, we don't know when something will happen. From that moment on we have two possibilities: either we go on just the same, or life is different for us. Some people are good in covering it up—too good. But this man from then on had an entirely different reaction to people. It was not a beloved one who gave him the ball, nor was it a beloved one to whom he gave it, and yet it made such an impact on him. Such moments are very, very full—full of possibility for us.

It's the whole question of approaching something, approaching somebody. Sharing something with them. Do you remember when you caught the hall and you grabbed it, and when you caught the ball and received it? This is a difference. And the same thing is with people. You can meet a person and grab the person—with looks or words or actions—or you can meet a person and really share something with them. That's the important thing—that you see it's not just in the active part but also in the reactive part in which it's so important to be there for it.

Now, let's say you are working together. For instance, one person puts a hand on another's shoulder. In other words, he's active, and in this being active he can allow his whole self to be there for it. He can also look out of the window, think about the weather, or the luncheon which comes very soon, maybe watch the other person intensely, or only give what is asked but not be fully there for the giving. The other person could receive it, but not entirely receive it—hold back a little. The one being touched feels his holding back, feels it and suffers with it. He does not in the moment allow the change which may open him more for what is being given to him. All these things will become more conscious as you become more awake.

The important thing about it is that often just a change of attitude can make a very great change. A change of your inner participation can make a great change in your outer participation. When you become sensitive in being with somebody else—either in receiving something or giving something so that you are not thinking about it or watching it—you are allowing from moment to moment your being more there for what is happening. And suppose that you have been touched, and after the class session you meet your co-students somewhere else. Does the sensitivity continue, or do you fall into the old way of non-relating? What Elsa Gindler taught me was to recognize the difference.

This attending to another person is not just holding his hand or his head, but it's meeting him and dealing with him and solving problems with him and whatever else there is which could become acute. It's in a way also a kind of handling—beautiful word, handling—another person, handling a situation. And the same thing which you have been doing literally with your hands yesterday, you can also translate into what you do when you speak with people, what you do when you listen to people, what you do when you see people.

Yesterday people have been working together who didn't know each other. This is a beautiful thing about our time together; and if it goes well nobody chooses, everybody works with the person who happens to be at hand. You could translate this also into your life when you meet people whom you don't know. Usually we kind of look at the person, measure the person up in many different ways. What is his social standing? Do I like her looks? How is he dressed? How does she come toward me? And so on. And accordingly, we react. There are people we like from the beginning, and there are people whom we dislike. And many people have the habit to quickly choose out of a group of people those with whom they "want to work," or "don't want to work," and so on.

Now, in this moment in which you get more loving, more sensitive, this would all gradually fall under the table. You would not be able to do this any more, because you would realize that everybody you meet is a human being, everybody has something to give to you and receive from you. In a way, that's what has brought me so close to Buddhism. Because in Buddhism one says, "Buddha is in everyone."

It may be possible, with the simple experiments which we do here, to get an attitude of more patience, more sensitivity, of not wanting immediate success, not wanting immediately that the person should be, so to say, custom-made for me. Astonishing things might happen between people who at first may not at all like each other. When it is possible for you to become so quiet and so unselective, so more human-to-human, you would understand very much more of the life which people have. Very often people come and they are full of anger and full of disappointment and full of frustration, and when you want to come into their neighborhood they reject you. It needs a great deal of patience and good feeling and willingness—if I may call it so, love—to gradually change this initial condition and relationship into one which might be more promising.

In New York City, for instance, we have the New School classes to which anybody comes, and often people are full of doubt, and I don't know what all. I remember one man who came to these classes, a very intelligent man, one who fought us every step of the way, sitting withdrawn all the time, and everything we said was right away rejected. In this class we worked and worked on very simple experiments, and by and by he opened up. He became interested enough to go with us to Monhegan and to Mexico. And he found among our students a nice young woman, and they married and each has since gone on to offer this work to others.

It was a terrific metamorphosis this man went through. He came loaded with suspicion and resentment. If he had been in an encounter group he might have screamed, but we did not invite him to scream. We gave him the occasion to experiment. And today he is a lovable, all-embracing person. You wouldn't believe what a change this kind of gradual trickling in of fuller feeling, of finer sensitivity, of more openness can bring about in the personality of someone who is willing to stick with it.

Personally, I do not believe that anybody should believe us. The more you doubt, the more you will find out that what this work offers has truth in it. It is through clean experimentation, through clean experience, that people learn what they gradually discover.

You can constantly work on this in your daily life. There is nothing in our daily life in which we could not become more open for what we do, could not become more reactive for what we do, and could not be cleaner in saying yes or no or perhaps to what we encounter. So that the "no" can be allowed entirely free, and the "perhaps" could be allowed entirely free, and the "yes" would not be conforming with society but something in which our inner—1 don't know how to call it—our inner indicator, or Buddha in you, or nature in you, can clearly tell you what you really, deeply inside feel is 'it', in how you have to respond to a situation when it offers itself to you.

We are all the time living

CHARLOTTE: Actually, everything which we happen to do is the same. It's a question of relating to whatever we do. We walk through the street, we step up to the sidewalk, come down to cross the street, go through a sunny spot and then a shady spot, and all the time we are communicating with ever-changing conditions. At any moment, just from step to step, or from breath to breath, or street to street, or task to task, or enjoyment to sorrow—whatever it is, we are all the time living We constantly have the chance to get in touch with people, with situations, with tasks, with anything which might come our way. That's why I say everything is the same.

And when you would work on only one thing fully and consistently you will learn the difference between being insensitive and becoming sensitive. Between allowing a connection or pushing things or people around, or holding back or giving yourself. There is no life activity, no life situation, no emotion, no thought which doesn't have the same invitation. So it doesn't really make any difference how or where you happen to get your experiences, because you will find the equivalent of what we have been doing with you here in anything you might do—if you will open your heart and your eyes and your senses, your subtleness, the intuition which we all have been ignoring a great deal in our lives. If you gradually get more and more open in this respect you will begin to feel that really everything is the same, is living.

There's the Zen saying: "Who can sit can do anything." You can also say, "Who can stand can do anything." Or, "Who can walk can do anything." You can allow the possibility to be just as sensitive and reactive to this 'anything' in any small compartment of your life. Some people reject cleaning dishes, for instance, which can be a top experience. Something wonderful to see all those dirty dishes asking, "Clean me! I want to be clean!" And you open the faucet and there's warm water, and you let the warm water flow over your hands, you feel it all through yourself. You take the first plate, and give it the chance to get warm, soapy water flowing over it, and you feel it getting cleaner. You hold it up and see the water dripping off it. You take a cloth and wipe it off, and you see it sparkle. Is it pottery, is it china, is it smooth, is it rough? You put the plate away on the shelf. You are in motion, you can feel space, air, the weight of the plate. Oh, endless drama! Your heart smiles.

You will find that anything is wonderful if you give it the chance to reveal itself to you. For instance, all the movements which you could allow at the typewriter. Instead of sitting and typing with tight shoulders and tighter arms, and pressing your ribs into the chair, and holding your legs, you could sit freely and you could move over the keys, and everything in you could be open for it just as much as when you dance. Actually it is a dance. So, everything in a way is a connection which you could either allow or you could deny—to the other and to yourself. When you allow it, you have an entirely different possibility of living.

I would like you to realize that what we happen to do in these few sessions is only one of the billions of things we could do instead—which offer themselves to you day and night, as long as you do not allow it to be taken for granted or say, "Oh, I know that already." Does anybody say, "I know how my breakfast tastes," before they eat it? Nobody knows, if we use our taste buds new. If we use our hands new. If we use our smell new. If you use everything new and fresh, you have from moment to moment a chance of renewed connection which is unique, and everything will look different. This is the delight of immediacy, because, if we allow this, we are all the time ready. I have no trouble 'getting high' when I'm allowing a real connection with things. So, I should suggest that you try it out for the next ten years and then write us a letter about how you feel!

It needs, of course, love, interest, curiosity—the sharpening of our equipment, which we have not been given by creation to be dormant but to be constantly exercised through life. So, this I'd like to give you: you can wear yourself out through daily living. You can always be against your nature—in sitting, in standing, in lying, in working, in speaking, in anything. You can press your voice out, or you can let it out. You can pound your feet on the floor until you get flat feet or you can touch the floor so that the feet get springy. You can stand and get a backache, or you can stand and get the most marvelous feeling of freshness. My teacher, Elsa Gindler, said, "A person can get heart disease by climbing a mountain, but also he can get rid of heart disease by climbing a mountain. It depends on how you climb." So in our life, we can sharpen our equipment by living—every moment—Whoomph! And we can also wear ourselves out. It depends on how we do it.

Serving creation

CHARLOTTE: So, I would like to invite you, when you are outside of class and in your everyday life, to let it be a time of awakening, whether you are in the kitchen or the fields or the office, whether you do something which needs great power, or something which need great refinement. Find out to which degree you can follow the messages inside, how the task wants to be done most directly and most easily.

The more you begin to be interested in this—the more that you come close to becoming more sensitive and more adjustable to what you are doing, the more you will find that it makes fun. It feels good. That's how the organism wants it, what creation has made you for. In other words, you serve creation—if you want to. You are not doing it as a duty; you are doing it as an inspiration.

I think we'll stop now, but I would like you to realize that we have been working on things which we do all the time. Nothing special. The difference is that we have not taken for granted that which is usually taken for granted, and therefore not cared for, you know. We have gone a little closer so it could be a little bit more fulfilled.

What I want to say at the end is: you have all kinds of activities which are constantly happening. You eat, you lift your food to your mouth and come down, you comb your hair, you brush your teeth, you do anything which belongs to daily living, and in all this you can practice. You can become more aware of when you are really allowing free contact with something or someone, and when you are constricting yourself and forcing something.

I wonder who likes this extension of consciousness? It's a demanding mistress, I tell you. It's not just an idea. Most people think it sounds very good—expanding consciousness—but when it comes to working it out, that's very different. You have just been getting a snatch of what it is like. The question is whether the bug bites. If it bites and continues to bite, you can say, "Aaaaah! I am on the way!" You can hide from it, you can run away from it, you can do anything, but it continues to bite. And that's how we develop.

THE END

Appendices: Class Sessions

The three class sessions reproduced here deal with a basic principle of Sensory Awareness: a conscious permissiveness to two forces of nature that determine our existence. These two forces are: (1) breathing and (2) our gravitational interaction with the magnetism of the earth. The experimentation is printed in italics; sequences of ellipsis points [. . . .] denote pauses of various lengths for silent working.

Appendix A: An experiment in being breathed

(From a workshop for everyone)
Third Los Angeles Seminar in Sensory Awareness
Sunday Afternoon, August 13, 1961
CHARLOTTE: I hope that the few experiments that we had before have been helpful for you to see your way a little bit clearer. Now I would like to give you a little hint about breathing. The way we are working with breathing is an absolutely spontaneous one. We are not teaching anybody how to breathe. In fact, the first thing (which often takes a great time to learn) is that a person who is finding out about breathing does not attempt to influence his breathing—the way he thinks it would be good. It is most difficult to bring into consciousness this function which is so much unconscious.

You have all probably noticed sometimes when you are just waking from sleep, or when you are sick in bed, or when you have a vacation, and are resting somewhere, that you have suddenly become conscious of your breathing. And you might have been peaceful enough, unanxious enough, to simply allow and enjoy what was. But most people, especially when they are in a class of instruction (I hope you don't call me an instructor!) have the feeling, as soon as it comes to something like breathing, that they have a duty. You have no duty whatsoever.

I agree that it's difficult to be so peaceful and undemanding that one would really be present in one's breathing activity—without influencing it—and just allow what comes to come, and what doesn't come not to come. In other words, the first thing when you are dealing with your breathing would be an ultimate casualness. Not staring at it and saying, "What are you doing?" Not saying to breathe deeply—or regularly. Nothing of that.

Just turn around and see in the garden how the wind is influencing the different leaves and trees. Do you see? It's perfectly different in every way. And after some time—for instance, right now—you would see it's different again. The motion is much more, a very little more, a little less and so on. So, in breathing, which is automatic, which is spontaneous, we have to be permissive to the fact that it is changing, that it is changeable. Breathing is as changeable as the weather. And the very character of it, or the very strength of it, is that it is changeable, so that when you run you breathe entirely differently. When you climb stairs, when you carry a package, when you sleep, when you are lying and resting—in all this, breathing is different. So please do not think there is any such a thing as "proper breathing."

I would like you now to lean back in your chairs, make yourselves entirely comfortable, and close your eyes. Don't jump on your breathing, but by and by something will begin to become conscious within you. . . . The important thing is to have patience, to have inner reverence, and not disturb it with your will. . . .

Just like your heartbeat, you let your breathing be as it wants to be. If it stops, let it stop. If it starts again, let it start again. If you have to sigh, sigh. If it gets fast, let it get fast. And if it leads you to a big yawn, allow it. Anything. . . . Don't try to watch it or observe it. You feel it anyhow. And while you are attending to the lovely activity right in you, I would like you—very, very gradually—to give up your leaning, and then come very gradually to sitting on the edge of your chair, without disturbing your breathing. . . .

I would like you just to feel the rhythms of your breathing, and anything that occurs, no matter how often there is change. To what degree is the inner of the organism alerted for what is happening? Do you feel any repercussions from your breathing within your organism? Where are you kind of moved insidely through your breathing? Is your inner already interested in it? . . .

I would like you—very gently, very gently—to place the palms of both your hands on the upper part of the chest. Very gently. And you just feel what happens underneath your hands. . . . Have your palms touch very gently—

not just the fingertips. And just feel what is happening underneath them. . . . If you can catch it, find out where else you feel anything of your breathing beside underneath your hands. Stay with your hands on your chest. . . .

And then you go very gently away—without disturbing the process, and see what you can feel without touching. . . . Could you be so that you are not "doing" your breathing anymore, but that you allow yourself to be breathed? . . .

Then once more go very gently to the same place and touch as fully as possible, as far as possible. Every finger is a feeler, and the palm is a feeler. And you feel how this touch influences your breathing. . . . Then I would like you to go away again—very gently—and continue to feel what is happening. . . .

Would you come to standing, without disturbing yourself at all. This time I would like you to touch the region of your diaphragm with both hands. . . . Allow every change in breathing that might want to come. . . . And again, very, very gently, your hands go away from there. Feel how it is without touching. Every spontaneous utterance is very welcome. . . .

Then go once more to the diaphragm with your hands—not the navel, not the abdomen, just the diaphragm. Although the hands are there, feel where in all your organism you feel breathing—besides where your hands are. . . .

Then go from there and touch all over the abdomen. Be open for it. Each finger is an independent agent. Use your hands freely, and independent of each other—not that you make a basket out of your hands, or anything like that. Just let your hands feel the breathing, on both right and left of the abdomen. . . . Then you go away with your hands, very gently, and feel what you are feeling now of your breathing. . . .

And at last I would like you to go with both of your hands on your head. Let them rest there very gently, and feel how this influences your breathing. . . . Then give yourself time to very gently go down with your arms, and continue to feel what happens in your breathing while you are going down. . . . Let your hands join in the back, so that the arms hang down, but the hands are joined. Feel how this influences your breathing. . . . Feel whether it is possible that you not observe it, not strain in your head for it, but allow the whole organism from the top of your head to your feet to be just sensitively open for what happens. Without an observing attitude. Open for what happens. . . . Let your hands gradually untwine and the arms come to hanging on both sides of your trunk. And give a moment's time for what is now. . . .

Who is a little bit more in contact with his breathing now?. . . This is the first beginning of a releasing. This is enough for now. Thank you very much.

END OF SESSION

Appendix B: Being permissive to gravity—the up-down tendency in every living creature

(From a workshop for experienced students)
Monhegan Island, Group III, Fifth Session
Thursday Morning, August 7, 1980

CHARLOTTE: Most peoples' lives are filled with going through motions. Who knows what I mean? And then, gradually, one begins to feel that this isn't 'it'. That's a very great moment. Don't begin to criticize yourself or feel you are no good. That's the moment in which you begin to become good, you know? You realize something, and then it's a question: "Do I get stuck in this realization, or does this realization bring about the future, what can be happening from now on?" For me, the real wonder is that when we realize something like that, we are surely led to something different where we are more present. And we don't have to make an effort for it. In the moment when we are really feeling it, it leads us on. Who has noticed it?

Suppose I want to embrace J. I have her in my arms, but not quite, you know? I feel, "Not quite!" Do I stay that way, or do I renew my embrace so that I feel, "Now I am really in touch with her!"? That's a beautiful possibility. I think this is the great wonder of the living organism, any living organism. For instance, these flowers—if you would see them through a microscope, you would find that in the very last bit of the outbranching edge of this flower, it flowers just the same as in the middle or anywhere else. Even in the little buds there is the same kind of inner strength, of juiciness, of flowering.

You know, each one of these plants has been going with their roots into the earth. They have been following the magnetism of the earth downward. But at the same time, they have been following the light upward. There is this "down" tendency and this "up" tendency in every living creature. This gives the possibility of opening and being. And they don't make any effort. Who understands that? The living being who is permissive to the forces of nature does not have to make efforts.

Now, this is not living. [*Charlotte holds up her microphone by the cord, and lets it dangle.*] This is what we call 'hanging'. . . . Ja, everything hangs. That means that whether it knows it or not, everything follows the pull of the earth, the magnetism of the earth. And that makes the cord as long as it is. Ja? . . . So, because the magnetism pulls, the cord comes to its full length: it hangs.

Now we have all those marvelous sensory nerves through our whole self, and we may be able to feel this pull on us. We are only able to feel the pull on us when we are not making an effort to hold ourselves upright. Because the very effort makes us insensitive to this fine invitation of the pull of the magnetism deep down in the earth. When I have my arm up in the air, and I hold it there with effort, I only feel the tension in my arm, but not the pull. Is that clear?

So, I would like us all to come up to standing, please. . . . How sensitized do we have to be to feel this pull—for instance, in our arms? . . . And then I would like you to feel how you have to change your standing so that this pull downward can be felt as simply as possible through you. . . . Where do your legs have to be so that the pull can go directly through you downward into the floor? . . . And how sensitive do we have to be in our whole interior so that we can experience this pull downward and let it happen? Don't fight against it. . . . Ja. Would you open your eyes, please.

[Charlotte stands with her legs wide apart and her arms held outward.] *When I stand like this do you think I can feel the pull downward? . . . No? Will you all stand like this, please. . . . Don't overdo. . . . What happens in the muscles so you can stand this way? . . . Who feels that the muscles are pretty occupied? And who feels that when you are standing like this, the pull goes through the air; it can't go through your legs? So, will you close your eyes and find out where in standing you have the feeling that your muscles are not occupied with holding, and you simply let the pull downward go through you.*

J, will you lie down, and offer me one of your legs? [J lies down and lifts one leg into the air, so that Charlotte can hold it and slap it.] *I take my partner's leg and lightly slap it all around until the strain has gone out of her. Then she lets that leg come down and raises the other so I can slap it. Will you all take a partner and do this to each other, please. . . .* [Sounds of slapping.] . . .

97

May I interrupt you a moment? Ones who are slapping, have the leg leaning against you so that you have everything there at your disposal. Ones who are lying, really offer your leg, and not let it lie morbidly in your partner's arms. [Slapping begins again.] . . . *When you feel it's enough, you gently let the leg come down to the floor so that the person who lies can continue to feel what your stimulation does to him or her. . . . Lying ones, sit up, and continue to feel what is still happening through what you have been receiving. . . . And you compare the condition of the leg which has been slapped with the other one. . . . Who is a little more intelligent in the one which has been slapped? A little more sensitized?*

So don't lose it when you lie down and offer your other leg. Please go up with your leg into the air so that your partner does not have to bend—to kneel down or anything like that. . . . [Slapping continues.] *All around! Back, front, side, inner, outer, everywhere! . . . Wake up! Wake up! . . . Not forgetting the foot, please; that's very important. . . . The back of the thigh, the back of the calf, everywhere. Just come to life! Get more feeling! . . . And then, very gently, when we finish slapping, we wait a moment so that there is not immediately a movement afterward—so there can be more drinking in of the influence of the slapping. And in letting the leg come down, we go so gently that the letting in and through can continue. . . . And those who have received the slapping, do you realize you have been given something? Are you still digesting? . . .*

Now, when you are coming up to standing, with your eyes closed, will you find a way of standing in which you have the feeling that the pull can go right through you. If possible, nobody looks down or sinks down, or any down, but just comes to a standing where you can be sensitive to the pull downward. . . . Who feels that one has to be very sensitive to become aware of the pull downward? It doesn't happen for everybody. . . . And when you don't feel it, you renew your standing until you get more of this fine feeling of this through-going permissiveness to the pull. . . .

And then the slappers lie down. Take your time. The important thing is that the person who lies has the time to first come to lying and then to offer the leg. . . . [Slapping continues.] . . . *No matter where you might slap now, are you there for the slapping? . . . And is the lying person there for the slapping? . . . Is there a real connection between the two of you? . . . Go as high as the leg is long, please. . . . And don't forget the foot from all sides. . . . When you feel it is enough, you gently let the leg come down. You carry it, but you let it come down there where it comes down by the pull of gravity. . . . Ja? . . . It's interesting to feel how the stimulation distributes through you. . . . Then, when the ones who have been slapped are so far as to offer their other leg, please do so. "Here I am!" . . . "Here I am!" . . . "Wake up, dear friend!" . . . Who says, "Thank you, thank you, thank you!"? . . .* [Slapping continues.]

When they feel it is enough, the slappers stop, and stay a little with the leg in their hand, or leaning against them, so that it can be still and taste in quiet what has happened. And when you have the feeling, "Now I can come down with this leg," you go so that the reactions to the stimulation are not being disturbed by your going too fast, or dropping, or whatever: The process can continue to go on. . . .

And then, all of us come up to standing—come again to a standing in which the pull can go right through us. . . . So, from the head through the neck, through everywhere where you exist, you would feel how you are under the influence of the pull. . . . And when you do not, you may have to change. . . . You know, in the two eyes, the two ears, two shoulders, two sides of your chest, two hips, two knees, two ankles, two feet—everywhere—is the possibility to let the weight through equally. That means the pull works in you. . . . And every change which is needed for this coming to more obedience to gravity is welcome. . . . Ja. . . . Thank you. Would you come closer, please, and sit down.

It isn't necessary that this will happen immediately, but it's possible that you will come a little closer to it. We are often still overloaded with holdings against gravity. And you may recognize this and maybe gradually give up a little more of the holding. Also, you might be able to feel when you are not letting it go through you. . . . **S**, would you give me one of those long poles? [*She holds the pole upright on the floor, and tips it at different angles.*] Is this standing? . . . Is this standing? . . . Is this standing? . . . Is this standing? . . [*Each time, students respond, "No!"*] . . . How do you know that this is not standing?

STUDENT: It feels like it's leaning. If you took your hand away, the pole would fall. [*Charlotte takes her hand away, and the pole falls.*]

CHARLOTTE: You know, my hand is like your muscles—which have to work overtime to keep you from falling. Of course, this pole is one solid piece of wood, and we are not one solid piece of wood. We are many, many, many joints and many, many, many muscles and ligaments and so on. Suppose you stand this way, with your pelvis forward and your chest backward. [*She illustrates.*] In order not to fall there must be muscles working to hold me. Many people stand like this all the time, so the muscles become tight all the time. That's how we create pains, all by ourselves. The nerves begin to say, "Ouch! I don't want that any more."

So, when your leg was slapped, who felt that when you bent it at the knee it wasn't quite so satisfying as when you really offered it in its full length? Many people stand like this—with bent knees—in order not to have stiff legs. But in standing one doesn't have to have stiff legs. And it's not a rule that the calves have to work hard, or that the knees have to lock, and so on and so on. One can stand so that the weight can go through the open tissues down to the ground. We come to this by feeling it out.

How is standing when my pelvis is forward and my chest backward? I feel a strain here in my lower back, and here in my shoulders, and in my knees; and the heels are pressed into the floor so that my feet cannot stand. So I change my way of standing very gradually until it feels, "Now the pull goes through me." Is that clear? Come up to standing, please. . . .

Now, everybody, for himself or herself, is going to slap the whole length of the legs and the feet. [Slapping begins.] . . . . *One moment!* [Slapping stops.] *It's not the strength of the slapping, but the quality of the slapping. You can have a great deal of tonicity in* piano. *You don't have to make it so fortissimo! Ja?* [Slapping begins again.] . . . *Don't forget your buttocks are part of it. . . . Wake up! Wake up! . . . Ja. . . . And when you feel it is enough, stop. And you close your eyes and just feel, "Where do I come closer to letting the weight through—not holding it up, but letting this pull on me through open tissues . . . so that I am coming to a standing which is . . . easy on the floor. . . . Give the possibility of a new coming to standing once in a while—to, perhaps, even allow it a little more, . . . so you are evenly balanced.*

Who realized that our feet are part of it? Are you standing on the floor, or are you lying on the floor with your feet? . . . Are you coming to standing on the floor, or do you press into your foot and not let the foot also stand on the floor? . . . Ja? . . . Who still has to allow changes until he comes to standing on the floor? What has to change—if something has to change? . . . Could you follow this sensation of need for change and renew your standing until you feel: "This is more it," that you are not hanging back anymore, even a little bit—but that you really come down: not backward, and not sideways. . . . but down? . . . A lot of giving to gravity also has to happen through the head and brain. . . So that this holding of the head can stop. . . . Ja. Would you sit down, please, and come a little closer.

We haven't yet spoken at all about our discoveries. Who feels that, to follow at all such a basic process, it is necessary to give up everything which has been learned—including from me and Charles? So you are, so to say, spick-and-span, fresh, . . . just following what you feel *now*. . . . And in discovering what I do *against* what is necessary, I can come closer to what is necessary—*in case* I'm not too vain or too idle. . . . You know? . . . Or do I still feel the obligation to do it right, right away? . . . Who understands that? In other words, you really have to become washed through of all that you *think* about—and just follow this . . . *force*. . . and feel how you can deal with it. Now, what did you discover?

STUDENT: As I was giving up my way of standing, I got very scared.

CHARLOTTE: What is your way of standing?

STUDENT: Not *coming* to standing, but just standing the way I'm used to.

CHARLOTTE: What is it you are "used to"?

STUDENT: What I *think* is "being easy in the knees," and "not making an effort to stand." And I was getting a glimpse of giving up the thinking and feeling it through. And then I caught myself being scared.

CHARLOTTE: Ja. Could you imagine that? Something new: we don't know yet! It's good when you get scared. You might wake up more for what you are at. . . . Ja?

STUDENT: Standing wasn't one thing; it was more of an endless journey. Every time I noticed one place that was holding, and it became a little easier, I immediately noticed another place that I hadn't noticed before, and by the time that had adjusted, the first one was back again. My attention went from my right knee to the outside of the foot, and then to my neck and shoulders and then down to my lower back. Each time some holding gave up I thought, "Oh, this is it—this is it." And it was, for a moment. But I never came to a place where I felt, "Finally, this is it! Here I can stay."

CHARLOTTE: Do you realize that she is busy with feeling easier? But that was not the task. The task was to find a possibility to follow the pull. Who understands the difference? Where does it lead me when I follow the pull? So I don't accept her translation into "Where can I be easier?"

STUDENT: "Easiness" in this case is my word for the feeling where I am not pulled either backward or forward by muscles that are holding me up against the pull of gravity.

CHARLOTTE: Ja. Anything else?

STUDENT: In my left side I felt I was very in touch with the ground and the magnetism of the earth that you spoke of. But I had a great deal of difficulty making connection with it on the right side. When I stood up the second time, the left side still felt grounded, but light. But there was something keeping me from making the connection here in my shoulder and arm.

CHARLOTTE: What I saw was that you were very much leaning backward; you weren't standing. . . . You didn't feel that yet? . . Someone else? Yes?

STUDENT: The first time I stood up, some words came to me: "Tree with a living core." And I realized that something was passing through the center of my legs that I was unaccustomed to feeling. I guess sensation switched from the muscles around my bones right through the bones. I really think I felt some ability for passage through that.

The second time I stood up I thought I felt energy—or weight, or gravity—going through to the floor. Then I was aware of parts of my body, like my shoulders or head, and I was playing with that. But for the moment I felt that one thing: "Tree with a living core."

CHARLOTTE: Gravity is very different from such an image. You have to be faithful to what you are doing. Otherwise you come into trouble. You go off into your ideas and you let your ideas lead you. Be very careful. As interesting as your ideas might be, leave them at home. Can you understand that?

STUDENT: The thing that first came was a feeling—and then, that image came to me, spontaneously. Now I'm beginning to think about it. But do you really consider that image a thought?

CHARLOTTE: Ja.

STUDENT: After we slapped our own legs the second time, I came back to standing and then I wanted to find another standing. I experimented with the feeling in my right leg, which I had slapped. Putting my right foot forward, my weight came more forward, and I came to another standing—and then another. When we sat down, I realized I had been so enjoying my adjustments, tasting my adjustments, . . . as this morning you spoke of continuing to eat because you like the taste of it. . . .

CHARLOTTE: K likes standing. . .

K, will you come forward, please. Sit down and give one of your legs to M. M, you take his foot in your hands, along the length of the sides so he can feel the sides. Ja. . . . And he feels how the foot is a continuation of the leg, . . . and whether it's possible to feel a direct continuation even from the head through the foot.

Would you all try this with each other, please. One offers a leg, and the other goes with the hands to both sides of the foot. You will have to bend your hands so that you are really at both sides of the foot, and don't touch the foot sole or the front of the foot. Just along the sides of the foot. . . . Let your partner really feel the continuity of herself or himself from top to bottom. . . .

Those whose feet are being held might lean backward, supported by your elbows or your hands on the floor. . . . If you are leaning backward, lean so that you have a free feeling all through yourself from your head down to the foot. . . . And when you have a real feeling of the sides of your foot, would you nod. Then your partner lets your foot come slowly down to the floor, . . . and the leg comes to lying on the floor. As your leg comes to lying, feel whether you can continue to exist in this inner connection from the top of the head down, including your feet. . . .

Will you come to standing now and feel whether you can allow this inner connection downward toward the floor in standing as well as in lying. . . . How do you have to contact the floor in order to permit this, . . . that you give up standing on your feet and you come to stand on the floor? . . . Who feels a difference in the two approaches to the floor?

Ja. Will you sit down, and get your other foot between your partner's two hands. . . . Those who offer their foot, offer themselves altogether. . . . And you feel how much life—and how much height—your foot has. . . . You might feel the architecture of your foot more: your toes, your heel, the instep, the arch.

. . . You know, when the foot becomes alive it's not a wooden plate. . . . It's formed by nature. . . .

So, after your partner's hands leave your foot, will you come up to standing once more. When you come to standing, permit this foot to exist and not press it so that it becomes a flat foot. Allow more of a standing on the floor and not into the floor. . . . So the weight can go through; and it's not in the ankle joint or the calf or the foot, but can be permitted through into the supporting basis. . . . Feel whether the distance between your feet is either too small or too big, so that the weight cannot go the simplest, the most direct way through to the floor. . . . And would you, while you are standing, feel whether your foot has any height. . . . Can you allow your foot to have life and height in connection with letting the weight through? . . . Or does it falter under the weight? Often one-thousandth of a millimeter makes the difference.

So, the others offer a leg. . . . This is something for you to try out for the next thirty years, you know. Who felt possibilities even now, I wonder— possibilities which you haven't known before? . . . Those whose foot is being held, wake up for your own alive structure, . . . without thinking what you have, . . . but just feeling, . . . and allowing the contact from head to foot. . . . Those who are holding a foot, are you with the person with whom you are working? Giving your own energy through the contact—not just being "touchy"—but really being in contact? . . . If possible, don't turn the foot to one side or the other, but allow the direct connection so that the person is not moved by you into another direction. . . . Then you gradually lower the leg. . . . And when you leave, those who are lying or leaning, please don't look, but just feel, "How is it when I permit this through-going feeling, this through-going sensitivity, and life?" . . . And then you come gently up to standing. . . . Ja. Who feels any effect of that what has been done, I wonder? . . .

So, will you come down to the floor again, and offer your other foot to your partner. . . . Who feels that hands, when they are quietly on both sides of the foot can be negligent, or can be really sensing? . . . Has this contact any influence on your breathing? . . . Does your partner's presence continue to influence you, even when you are not in touch any more? . . .

So, when you are ready for it, come up to standing and find out how it is now. This includes everybody, please. . . . Is there such a thing as being on the floor and not into the floor? So that the pull can go through me, all through me freely, and make me stand? . . . Every instinctive need of fine changes toward the floor are very welcome, you know. You must trust your instinct. When it isn't quite it, maybe when you change a little it becomes more it. Just giving yourself a chance. . . . Ja.

Now two other people come together. R, will you sit down and give me one of your legs? . . This time you don't stay just touching the foot, but you very clearly slap the two sides of the foot until it gets very awake! [Charlotte demonstrates.] The one who receives the slapping does not lean back and say, "Oh, yes, she does it for me." You know? But you are keenly with it! That means, "Wake up, dear friend!" [Slapping begins.] . . . . Are you already a little more awake? Ja? Good! . . . What does your breathing say to it? . . . Both sides equally. Use both your hands, ... on the sides of the heels, everywhere, just as clear as possible. . . . Wake up! . . . And then when you stop slapping, gently let the leg down without disturbing the reactions which might come. . . .

This has, I hope, benefitted you all the way through, particularly in your brain. That you are letting it through, and not keeping your head out of the experience, Ja? Then you offer your other leg. . . . Everywhere in you is the possibility of being, receiving what is done down there. . . . Some people may feel, "Why don't you use your fist? I'm not made of . . . glass. . . . In other words, don't hesitate. There are bones which like to be waked up, and tissue that likes to be waked up, Ja? . . . Then we stop and our dear friends come up to standing and find out how standing is now. . . . What is acute in this moment of my life? How is the connection downward? . . . How does it want to be now, when I follow the pull in being open to it? . . . Who was interested in this, I wonder? . . . Ja.

So, will you serve your partner who was so nice to you. . . . The heel is also exposed for the slapping. . . . And the sides of the toes—but only the sides. Little toe and big toe—on both sides. . . . Wake up all the length through. . . . Ja. Do you feel the architecture there where you slap? Where it is broader, and where it's most slender, and so on and so on? . . . Ja. We stop and let our partner stay under the influence while we are placing the leg down on the floor. . . . Then the other leg is offered, . . . just the sides. . . . Who feels there are bones? Influence the bone and the tissue. Go through with the tapping, in right there. "Wake up! Wake up!" . . . And when you feel it's enough, you stop. . . . And you come down with the leg of your partner. . . . The people who are lying may be very eager to come up to standing to find out, "What is it doing to me now?" So, as soon as you are ready, come up. . . .

Who is curious? . . . With eyes closed, you orient yourself downward, feeling what it is to come to more standing on this ground . . to letting weight through more fully . . . and staying awake everywhere. . . . I would like everybody to come up and walk—and find out, "How does it feel in walking?" Just give yourself a little chance. . . . Walk a little faster, please. . . . "How do I let this pull through in walking? . . . And what helps me not to succumb to the pull, but simply permit it to influence me?". . .

In feeling this inner possibility of being alive, would you come once more to a new standing—and feel how you can permit what is needed in standing when you are more conscious of what is needed inside. . . . It's a kind of going into unknown territory—just finding out, "How does it want to be in me now, when I'm a little more reactive to what is needed for standing—not in my old way but . . . elastically? . . . When I'm not hanging backward over my back, nor hanging forward over my front, but finding my balance over front and back?" . . . And when you have the feeling, "This is as close as I can come," will you raise you hand again? . . . Ja? . . . Who feels it is a very subtle thing? . . . Mmm-hmm. Ja. . . .

Who realizes that everybody has the possibility to work on this at any time? Who has a floor—a rug, a piece of meadow . . . to stand on, . . . to lie on, . . . to walk over? . . . And air to breathe? . . . So, I think that is enough for today. Thank you very much.

END OF SESSION

Monhegan Island, Group III, Sixth Session
Friday Morning, August 8, 1980

CHARLOTTE: Who would like to speak out about yesterday? Ja?

STUDENT: I noticed a change in the way I walked. I felt much lighter.

CHARLOTTE: That is astonishing from this little bit of change. You know, when something which is unawake becomes awake and gets more vitality, that means your whole person wakes up. Stepping is not just a matter of a foot. It seemingly has been going through you. . . . Anything else?

STUDENT: This morning I felt very grateful, and I was dancing and feeling the wet grass, and all of a sudden I found myself wanting to stand on my head. Once I was up there, I got in touch with the height of me in a different way. As I came down I realized I hadn't stood on my head for two years, since I had back problems.

CHARLOTTE: Uh-huh. So it just happened because you liked to do it. Do you have the feeling it had something to do with our experiment in coming more to standing? . . . Because you spoke of height. . . . In standing on the head, it's a question of how gravity goes through one. When one is a little too much backward or forward, one has to work one's muscles very much to stay up. But when one is more in the middle, then the muscles opposite are, so to say, balancing one—and it feels easy. In the moment in which one is in balance, that is always the sign. The closer one comes to balance, the more easy it feels. The more life it feels, also.

I would suggest you come up to standing, and maybe we close our eyes. First give a little time to gradually get a little more awake throughout yourself. . . . Of course, whatever is necessary for little changes in standing is invited. . . . And, in the way you are touching the floor, would you feel where the weight goes through to the floor, whether it's more toward the heels, or toward the ball of the foot. . . . Who feels it is more forward? . . . Who feels it is more backward? . . . Uh-huh. Who feels it is more toward the middle? . . . Ja.

Now I would suggest that, with your eyes closed, you allow a little gentle swaying on the floor—a very little. You can stay perfectly quiet without bending in any way in your hips or in your chest, or so. Just feel how it is when

107

you come gradually a little more forward. And how it feels when you come a little more backward. . . . So you just get the impression of the change in weight distribution, . . . and whatever you feel has an influence on your tissue when you come forward. . . . And what's happening in the musculature when you come backward. . . . The important thing is that you allow this swaying quite confidently. . . . Who likes to sway a little? . . . Mm-hmm. So it comes by itself, in case you are ready for it. . . . And the less you observe it, the better you will feel it. . . . What happens when you come more and more backward? . . . And what happens when you go through the middle and come gradually more and more forward? . . . Who feels that it influences the musculature very differently? Take a little time for it, . . . so your ankle joints are elastic, so that you can allow the sway. . . .

Now, would you interrupt the swaying, and everybody slaps his legs, one leg after the other, to renew. . . . The back of your thighs, the knees, the calves, the buttocks, . . . everything. . . . And then sit down for a moment.

Who could feel something of the change in weight distribution? . . . Who could feel something of an influence on the musculature? . . . Uh-huh. Isn't it wonderful that we have muscles?! . . . That's what we have as security measures. If you wouldn't have them, you would fall. It's very interesting to feel the changes that happen. . . *naturally,* . . . you know. So, did anybody feel what happened in coming forward?

STUDENT: When I came forward my knees locked, very tight, like they were trying to keep me up.

STUDENT: When I came forward, my toes gripped the floor, and my inner calves tightened.

CHARLOTTE: Yes. They help you, Ja? Otherwise you would have fallen. . . . Anything else?

STUDENT: I felt a lot of movement at the very bottom of my spine. I had a little pain there when I moved forward. I felt it stretched out right there.

STUDENT: When I came forward I felt a tightness through the shoulder and neck muscles; and I thought it was peculiar that I would be holding myself up by my neck

CHARLOTTE: Ja. Of course that is "extra."

STUDENT: It *felt* extra.

STUDENT: I felt something in my jaw, as I went back and forth.

Charlotte: Ja. How about backward?

Student: I felt it was really frightening—like I could only go so far back and then I was going to fall over. I could hardly go at all. And there was a lot of tightness in my upper back . . . and the back of my neck and head. And the more frightening it was, the more tightness there was.

Charlotte: Don't go so far that you get afraid.

Student: But I was hardly going back far at all!

Student: When I went back, I realized that that's where I am most of the time. And then, in order to stay there, I have to create a sort of wall behind myself, and I do that by raising my shoulders and back. And when I began to move forward, I felt that my shoulders just wanted to drop. There was no reason why they had to be up there any more. I felt myself come under myself—so that my legs started to relax and I felt that I was very, very far forward, when all I had done was come a little bit forward.

Charlotte: Who feels how very big even small movements are when one goes gently and really feels them? Even when they are *so* small they feel endless?

Student: I also got frightened in going back. I felt it was very easy to go forward and stay all of a piece; but when I went backward I felt a break, a bending, at my hips, so that I could keep my chest and head somehow forward, and not risk their weight pulling me back.

Charlotte: But that was the task: to lean without bending. . . . So, you went too far backward for your possibilities.

Student: And, through the whole thing, I was aware of the weight of my head and my shoulders being what I had to balance in going back and forth. It seemed reasonably easy to go backward and forward down to the hips. But I had to be very aware of where my head was or the weight of the head would carry me too far forward or back. Maybe that was my *idea* of it.

Charlotte: Ja: the *idea* of it.

Would you all take a pole, please. [Each pole is more than six feet long.] *. . . Now, two people come together, and stand opposite one another. One has the hands some place on the pole, and the other has the hands somewhere else on the pole. The pole stays standing on the floor, and you let it come a little forward and backward. Can you feel—when you are not holding the pole* very tightly—that it is very moveable on the floor, that it easily goes back and forth? It goes with you immediately. So, will you try it out, please. . . . Swaying a little forward, and swaying a little backward, and the pole goes with you. . . .

And you go so gently, so gently, that you can feel how the weight goes through you into the floor—and where it is where you feel the lightest. . . . Be very careful that you don't hang your head backward. . . . You follow the experiment as a standing person. . . . Where is it easiest in standing? . . . When somebody feels, "Here, it is easiest," he or she says very gently, "Here," and the partner feels whether it is the same. . . . [Occasionally someone says, "Here."] . . . And where you feel, "Here it feels easiest," you stay there, and you feel where you are then. . . . Who feels that allowing the change of weight on the floor is interesting: to feel how it is when your weight goes through the heels; or more weight comes forward; and how it is when your weight goes through the middle; and so on? . . . When you come to the place where it is easiest, just raise your hand for a moment. . . .

Ja. Thank you. Slap your feet and ankle joints once more, please. . . . Maybe your calves also. . . . Ja, so they really live. . . .

So now, when you have the pole standing on the floor—not in the air: on the floor—the important thing is that your pole is not pressed into the floor. And you don't hold yourself up with it; you only have it as a teacher, Ja? What happens to the pole you could perhaps allow to happen to you. We'll try it out once more. . . .

So, we close our eyes and we just stand for a moment quietly, and feel if the pole is so easy to our touch that it's easy on the floor. . . . Then it will start by itself. . . . There are fine changes in the musculature that you can begin to feel. . . . And once in a while, when you come where standing feels lightest, you stay. . . . It's very interesting to feel how weight distributes itself gradually more and more, or less and less, . . . where you feel there is more muscle work involved, and where you feel it isn't necessary any more. . . . And maybe, by and by, we can feel the change in the musculature when [the muscle work] is needed or not needed, and we will be able to give up the tendency to hold when it's not necessary. . . . And when you come to a place where you feel standing is really the easiest, you stay there for a while—staying easy, not holding yourself there. . . . And you feel where you are right now. . . . When I am where it's easiest, am I somewhere toward the heels or toward the toes,

or where? . . . Even in going sideways, find the easiest way. . . . Who feels that
you have to go gradually—otherwise one can't feel it? . . .

So, thank you very much. Everybody lies down. . . . When you are coming
to lying now, where is the most even distribution of weight in lying on this
ground, . . . so that everything inside can be equally satisfied? . . . It's up to us
to allow it. . . .

Yes. . . . When you are so far, come up again to standing, please, this
time without poles. . . . I would like you to bring your hands in the region of
your lower chest. Try swaying once more, forward and backward, but very
gradually so you can feel it more. . . . When you have your hands on your
chest, would you feel whether you are extending yourself there, or whether you
are just at peace there. You are not trying to extend your front. If you do, give
it up; give up the extending. . . . Let your hands come down whenever you like
to change. . . . When you come up with your hands again, feel whether you
can come up without extending your front, just being in comfort and allowing
this gentle swaying. . . . Where is the easiest place? . . . And coming back to
the lower chest, . . . can you just be easy, . . . no pull on your lungs, nor your
stomach, nor on your heart? . . . Can all that is located inside be easy? . . .

And when you feel your breathing, would you, without pulling on yourself,
feel how elastic your tissues are for even the slightest bit of breathing. . . . Ja? . . .
When you go up again with your hands, be gentle; feel, "Must I extend
myself, or can I stay at ease in my inner organs, . . . so that the weight can go
right through, downward, and is not held up by pushing myself upward?" . . .
When you find the easiest place, stay there for a little while, and just feel
whether you can let the feeling of weight distribution right down into the
ground—without pushing yourself. . . . And when you remove your hands,
and your arms come down, can you continue in this allowing downward . . . so
that the whole organism is open downward—it's not held up in the middle? . . .
Would you just turn around a little—gently—and see how everybody is
standing. . . . Ja. Come forward please, and sit down. . . .

CHARLOTTE: Was there anything you saw when the people were all
standing? . . . Did it in any way impress you, seeing the people standing?

STUDENT: Everybody looked more peaceful, and everybody was standing
in a different way. I know each person, and . . . they were so different!

CHARLOTTE: Isn't that strange? Who realized it, too? . . . What was
happening? Did you feel any influence from this whole procedure? It

111

was a long way that we went, trying something out. Everything had to do with weight distribution. That means—downward. Has anybody anything to say about it? . . . Ja?

STUDENT: Yesterday when we were walking, what was important was the feel of the floor under my feet: It felt very soft and welcoming, and yet, as my foot came down, there was all the support in the world to let me walk on. Today, when we were working with the poles, what was most powerful was feeling that connection to the floor, and where my feet met it. What happened above my feet seemed to be in response to how much of my foot sole was in contact with the floor, and where it was in contact. I found that's where my weight goes through, and the slightest change in that connection is what everything else in me responds to.

When we were moving with the poles frontward and backward, it was interesting. But when we went sideways I realized that I still don't give my weight to my left leg—the one that I broke. I thought I did. I can stand on my left leg, and I thought I was giving my full weight. But even when I thought I had given as much weight to my left as to my right, I found that the weight of the pole against my fingers was still on the right side. . . . And when I allowed myself to go over to the left, and give the amount of weight that evidently was equal, I felt in my right leg the overwork-tension that kept me from feeling what was happening in it.

CHARLOTTE: Mm-hmm. Who felt also that we often keep something which has become unnecessary? And this is not only in the change of weight distribution, but often in so many things in our living—to keep on with something although the need for it is long past? Ja?

STUDENT: I became very aware of a lot of pain and tension in my pelvic and lower back area.

CHARLOTTE: At last! Could you feel what created it?

STUDENT: For one second, I experienced this real pleasure going through me as I found just the right spot in standing. And it felt so easy to be there. And yet I realized how much of me I put outside myself. I was thinking I wanted to look in a mirror, rather than, you know, *feel* it—to *see* how it looked.

CHARLOTTE: Ja. Who knows that? One is ahead of oneself! You want a little more, Ja? There was a wonderful article in *The New York Times* the other day by a man who writes of the American Dream. Who has read it? One always wants more. One is always looking to the future for more. What *is* is never enough—although it's very much enough. But it is never enough because he's always ahead of himself. That's the American Dream. . . . Be careful! . . Ja?

STUDENT: When you told me to let go of thinking of my head, I became aware of my feet in the adjustment of the weight. And I found that each time that I came to the right spot, I felt a release in my loin and bottom.

CHARLOTTE: You didn't have to hold there anymore.

STUDENT: I wasn't aware of holding again as I started to move, but each time I came to the right spot there was a release in my whole bottom. The second time it happened, I tried to notice when in the movement I tightened.

CHARLOTTE: Okay. Where was what she calls "the right spot?" Where was it? That's the question. Could anybody say where you happened to be when it felt best? Did you feel there was somewhere it was easiest?

STUDENT: There were several instances where I felt the beginning of the easy lightness, and as soon as my mind recognized it, that would throw me off.

CHARLOTTE: Ja. Who feels that, in order to find out about something like this we need *utter* inner quiet? So, we are not watching. We are all *here*, all sensing, you know? The sensitivity extends everywhere, and one doesn't have to watch.

STUDENT: I had an amazing discovery—after thirty-one years of working! I got to a spot where I thought, "Oh, this is it, this is marvelous!" We were moving from side to side. And then I started to move toward the left, and my left leg said, "No, this is it!" And I got completely confused and had to change my standing completely. I thought it was it—on the right side. But I didn't realize the left leg wasn't standing. I could not find a point. What I found was a place where I felt as though I was vibrating. And I could feel the vibration, but it never felt like one point.

CHARLOTTE: Ja, the question is where were you when—

STUDENT: When I was just vibrating? I don't know.

CHARLOTTE: Okay. It doesn't make the least difference whether you found it or not. Who enjoyed the swaying, I wonder? You know, it's a wonderful way of meditation—wonderful—to really give yourself to this! And by and by you will recognize more.

STUDENT: When I felt I was near the place, I felt a delicious kind of freedom in my breathing. It just arrived.

CHARLOTTE: Um-hmm. Yes. You know, when you are coming more to the side, since the weight distributes, of course you feel more weight there. And the muscles begin to respond to that—that is only natural. In other words, when you feel something happening in the musculature—that means functioning. (Unless you strain and hold, and I'm not speaking of straining.) So there is nothing right or wrong about it—it's only so.

I would like everybody to lie down on the stomach. . . . Would you turn your head so that you can lie on one cheek, or one ear, but otherwise well distributed all over. So, instead of lying on your back this time, you are lying with your front on the floor. . . . I wonder whether you have any sensations of happenings throughout you which have to do with your inner functioning? . . . Any movement through you? . . . Can you feel any response in your musculature to these movements? Does it give to these movements? . . . And when you feel that here or there it doesn't give, that it's holding against the movement maybe you can allow a little change so that the ways of these movements can be more open. . . .

Do you have the feeling that the floor can feel any of your movements? . . . Is there any openness in your functioning toward the ground on which you are lying? . . . Would you feel whether you have overstretched yourself here or there in lying? Perhaps you don't need so much space in your stomach or your belly, and you would have to change a little so that you are not over-stretching yourself. . . . When you feel you need a little more room inside here or there for these inner movements, maybe by and by you can permit it. . . . And then I would suggest that you feel whether there are also inner movements going through your inner back—room through the back of your head or neck or shoulder girdle, back of the chest and waist, back of the pelvis, until down toward the legs. . . . Do you have the feeling that you are open for these inner movements in your back? . . . And could you become a little more awake in your tissue through your back for these inner movements? . . .

Has it, perhaps, anything to do with breathing? . . . Has it, perhaps, anything to do with the air around you? Around your back? . . . And would you now feel how these movements go and extend toward the back and the front at the same time. . . . Or, better, what moves in you in all directions? . . . So, when you have felt this a little more, I would like you, with your eyelids closed, to come gently up to standing. Would it be possible to feel how standing wants to be when you would permit these inner movements to influence you equally toward front and back . . . so nothing is preferred? . . . Always staying faithful to these inner activities, and allowing a standing which doesn't close you up somewhere and overextend you somewhere else. . . . Where would I land in standing . . . so I would be just as elastic to the inner movements in back and front . . . equally? . . . It may be a standing which you have never experienced before. So, follow only your sensations. . . . Where is it most refinedly responsive to what is happening inside? . . . When you have found this, raise your hand, please. . . . Ja. . . . For whom is it different from the usual way you stand? . . . Mm-hmm. Ja. . . . And without watching, maybe you feel what is different—in case it is. . . .

Open your eyes, please, and two people come together; so everybody has a partner. . . . One goes on four legs and is slapped by the partner, starting out at the very bottom where the coccyx is, and the buttocks. [Charlotte demonstrates.] *. . . And you go along the spine and land with your tapping at the top of the head. All along the spine. Wake up the whole spinal area.*

[General tapping begins.] *. . . Just the spine, in the middle, you know. Those who are on their four legs may have to change a little bit to be more welcoming to the tapping. And it may be that the inner mobility also may become more alerted for the tapping. . . . And when the others have tapped very fully, will they stand with their partner between their legs and tap both sides of their friend, from the hips up to the armpits. Yes? . . . And again, the tapping means, "Wake up, dear friend, wake up inside! How about your inner activity becoming a little aware of the fact that you exist?" . . . .*

Then you stop and step back, and the kneeling people stay for a moment and feel how this is now with regard to this question of letting inner movement through. . . . And with that in their senses, would they come up to standing and feel how this influences their standing now. . . . If possible, not landing right away in an habitual standing, but feeling out, "What does it want from me, now? . . . Do I allow space for inner elasticity through back and sides? . . . And where am I now when I allow this a little more?" . . . . Ja? . . .

So, the others are coming down now. Tappers, be sure you go along the spine, and along the back of the head to the top of the head—all along the middle of the back. . . . [Tapping begins again.] *If the ones being tapped have to allow changes for what their friend does to them, please be as welcoming as possible.* . . . *Wake up! Wake up inside! Allow the changes.* . . . *When the tappers feel it's enough, they stop* . . . *and let the others just feel how this already affects their inner awakeness.* . . . *Then they step over their friend, and slap both sides. No beating, please—slapping!* . . . *So it can really penetrate.* . . . *Wake up, dear friends!* . . .

Then you stop, and everybody goes on four legs. . . . *Would you feel whether you could allow more even distribution of inner activity through you* . . . *in becoming more elastic for it in the musculature around your framework and around your organic functioning.* . . . *If I'm armored with holding somewhere, I can give a little. Where I'm too contracted, I can open up—and so on. So you serve what is needed inside.* . . .

Would you all go gently on your elbows, so that your forearms lie on the floor. When you are a little lower this way, can you perhaps feel a little more of how much room you need inside for the space your inner activities want to occupy? . . . *Even in the back of your neck and in your head, are you elastic for what is needed to go through and out?* . . .

And with this, you come up. Don't allow the way up to destroy what has happened in you. Come up and perhaps find a new standing, obedient to what it wants from you inside. . . . *The back is not "a bone," but about twenty-five bones. No—many more!* . . . *It's not a wooden plate which is hard and upright, but something elastic which can give.* . . . *Nothing has to be held, but can come to open possibility for the inner activities.* . . . *If you allow this more, where do you land in standing?* . . .

Would you once more place your hands on your lower chest, and feel whether you are still holding it up, or whether it can be peaceful there—able to respond to the inner activity rather than be held up. . . . *Ja.* . . . *And could you permit what comes by itself,* . . . *instead of creating it.* . . . *So, when you lie down once more, just be interested in what comes by itself. And when you feel you create something, you might be able to give up this creating, which is unnecessary.* . . .

So, come down to lying on your back. . . . *This time I would suggest that everybody places their feet on the floor so that the knees are bent. Find a place for your feet where the legs can stand freely. . . . You can feel whether your rib cage and your pelvis and shoulder girdle and so on can be easily adjusted to the floor as well as to your inner activities . . . . so that a really good, comfortable contact is permitted. . . . And we once again put our hands on our lower chest. Just feel what's happening inside. . . . I say "happening," not what "is done" inside. . . . What is happening inside from moment to moment? . . . It may change. . . .*

So, you have two ways of being touched. One is that your hand touches you, and the other is that the floor touches you. And in between is you. . . . Who feels that one can feel without having to watch? . . . So you go a little lower with your hands, toward the diaphragm . . . and you take a little time to feel what's happening between your hands and the floor in this area. . . . And you go still a little lower toward the belly . . . and you feel what's happening there between your hands and the floor. . . . And then you go with your hands as low as is possible in your trunk, feeling what happens there between floor and hands. . . . Go so low that you are in the neighborhood of your legs, but still on your trunk. . . .

Would you then go with both of your hands on top of each other, and gently cover your forehead. . . . Take a little time to feel what's happening there between your hands and the floor. . . . And at last you place your hands on your very upper chest. Open them fully so you have the possibility to feel a lot of territory. And, again, you feel what's happening between your hands and the floor. . . . And when you now remove your hands, and you don't any more touch any area in your front, would you feel what's happening in you . . . in terms of inner activity . . . while you are lying in contact with the floor and, hopefully, with the air around you. . . .

END OF SESSION

Appendix C: Gravity, space, and energy

(From the third session of a joint workshop with Allan Watts, ca. 1962, in Sausalito, California)

CHARLOTTE: The discussion of [gravity] and space has interested me very much. And there was another thing which we touched very lightly yesterday—the question of energy. You remember that, before we started to work, we discussed what happens in a healthy process of recovery, of giving up inhibitions and coming to regeneration. No real regeneration can happen without the restrictions getting less at the same time, so that the processes in the organism which make for rebalancing and recovery are allowed to start.

It's hard to put it, but this all has to do with the question of space, and Alan spoke of weight. Let's say that we are tissue which is of a certain denseness, which is exposed to the pull of the earth. It is a very fascinating thing that from deep down in the middle of the earth there is a magnetic pull on us which keeps us from flying off. If we didn't have this pull on us everybody would be somewhere [out] in the cosmos. Through this fine pull we stay on earth. But if we are too loaded with energy, we can't feel it. When we have just the amount of energy to be [really] lying or standing or sitting or walking—and we are awake innerly—then we can feel this fine pull.

And it has an absolutely bewitching quality. It asks you, "Come, follow me." That means, "Be comfortable; this is the way." When we give to the pull, we come much more to comfort. But when our organism—or that of flowers or animals that are sick—has not enough energy, then this pull is able to deplete us further. Then we can be in a state in which the pull of the earth can make us absolutely sluggish. In the fall, when the trees don't have so much juice any more and the energy doesn't go to the ends of the branches and to the leaves, there comes a moment when the leaves fall. They just fall off—are pulled off by the pull of the earth. And then gravity begins to pull what was formerly a leaf down into the earth, and by and by it becomes earth. And out of that comes new life. It's a magnificent circle which includes everything.

Now, this pull [of gravity] is on every human being. But something fabulous happens: at the same time it is pulling us downward, this pull invites the processes within the organism to pick up. There is an answer to the pull: it creates energy.

I'm speaking always of functioning, living material. [For instance,] the pull [downward] is always working on the trees. And, at the same time, the trees pull up out of the earth the juices which go up the trees and fill them to the remotest ends, so that the last leaf on the tree is just as full of energy as any other leaf. So, there is this constant counter-play: the pull of the earth creates energy, and when the energy is just equal to the pull of the earth, then we are in balance. When we are in balance, we get, strangely enough, this feeling of space. Who has noticed that, sometimes? It's very strange. And we also get the feeling of an interaction between weight and energy which creates lightness.

Of course this is not just to be explained in terms of physical processes—cosmic processes, if you want it so. It can also be explained from a different side. You know how a person looks if he is disinterested: he droops. He isn't reactive. He gets sluggish. As soon as such a sluggish person notices something which begins to interest him, then he begins to pick up. That means that he comes up and soon enough you see that his features begin to fill up and then he sits differently and then he breathes differently and his whole inner countenance changes. And, of course, in a state of great inspiration and great contact with things, this condition of balance and energy—just the right condition, not too much and not too little, but just right—is always present. You can, when you look at the person, see the way he carries himself: whether he is interested or not, whether he is elated or not, whether he is inspired or not, whether he is bored or not. You see this right away. You only don't translate it into the fabulous inner happiness.

Now, we are more-or-less unconscious of these things. And I would like to warn you: once you know such things, you begin to work for them. But you can't work for them in the sense that you would say to yourself, "Now I'm going to be very energetic!" Very often when we work on breathing and I trust very much that a person will begin to sense what's happening, he begins to make an effort to breathe. He begins to control his breathing and form his breathing, which, of course, has nothing to do with the spontaneous emergence of some kind of more inner reactiveness. So, it's much better that you forget everything. Then what happens, happens. What did you say, Alan, about spontaneity? "You can't be purposeful, and at the same time spontaneous. It has to be one or the other."

So, I wanted very much to work with you today on this very delicate subject matter. There are many people who are used to holding themselves up by pure muscle power, because otherwise they would be utterly drooping. But inside they are hollow. It would probably be better if they would be drooping, because holding themselves up is a pure lie. I mean, it is not supported by an inner vitality.

We have millions of little alive organisms within us who all need space, and on account of that people pull themselves up with their muscle power when actually inside they are [nearly] lifeless. They would have to go the opposite way; they would first have to become honest. That means that they would have to allow their true state to come out. As long as they don't allow this, they cannot expect any change in any way—because nature does not touch anything that is untrue. It just turns its head away. So, when one is drooping, one allows it fully. And then there comes a moment in which one can't stand it any more. And then you come to a state of inner balance and health, or whatever you want to call it, in which the rhythms of natural life build you out—not your will which forces your muscles into pulling you up from the outside.

So, I would like you to come up to standing. And would you—as you are so quietly standing—feel out how your organism is charged from the inside, including the head. Don't let anything not belong to your organism. Through your hair and through to underneath your footsoles, permit yourself to exist. . . .

I would like you to allow your arms to be free, to be freely hanging so that you also allow life in them, not flabbiness. Feel whether you could allow your arms and your hands to become alive so that they don't hang like chains from you, but are a part of you. . . .

Would you notice whether you can feel how you occupy space just by standing. . . .

And those of you who pull yourselves up, very gradually give this up— very gradually, so that you come to an experience of the space which is truly you, without [that kind of] pull. . . .

And I would like you, as you are standing quietly, to see what you can sense of any processes of life going through you—and how they build you. Also where they bring you in coming to standing. . . .

So, I would like you to feel the rhythms of life in yourself. For instance, have you any sensation of any energy currents going through you? Is there any sign of a circulation which goes through you? Do you give occasion through your own—let me say—inviting attitude so that the circulation can easily go through? . . .

And without making any fuss about it, without consciously trying to change it at all, can you feel anything of your breathing? And has your breathing anything to do with the way you stand? . . .

And what else of rhythms or currents, or whatever it is, do you feel happening in yourself as you are standing in this way? Please don't watch, but just expose yourself to what happens. . . .

So, you are standing now quietly for some while. And I would like to ask you, "Is there in any way a sensation of movement? Is there a sensation of rhythm—even when you are quiet? Just feel yourself from downward—from the earth—all through, through the whole space from where you start to where you end. . . .

The End

About the Author

The teachings of Charlotte Selver, the founder in the U.S. of Sensory Awareness, are preserved almost exclusively as audio tapes of her many classes. In the late 1970s she entrusted Mr. Littlewood with the monumental task of turning those tapes into a book of her classroom interactions. It is her voice that speaks to the reader from these pages.

Bill Littlewood studied for years with Charlotte Selver and served for a year or so as editor of the Bulletins of the Sensory Awareness Foundation. For shepherding to completion the first book about Selver's work, *Sensory Awareness: The Rediscovery of Experiencing*, he received praise and gratitude from its author, Charles Brooks, "for tempering the alloy from which this instrument was forged."

Mary Alice Roche, a long-time student of Charlotte Selver, wrote extensively on Sensory Awareness and other topics. She helped found the Sensory Awareness Foundation in 1971, became its first archivist, and edited most of its Bulletins. She died in July 2004, having spent the last months of her life guiding to publication the manuscript of *Waking Up*.